Trial By Fire
A Tale of Two Houses
Doug Rucker

TRIAL BY FIRE
A Tale of Two Houses
Layout by Helane Freeman

Copyright © 2016 Doug Rucker
All rights reserved.

Doug Rucker
Vilimapubco
Malibu, CA
ruckerdoug@gmail.com

No part of this publication may be reproduced, distributed, or transmitted in any form or by any means, including photocopying, recording, or other electronic or mechanical methods, without the prior written permission of the publisher, except in the case of brief quotations embodied in critical reviews and certain other noncommercial uses permitted by copyright law.

For permission requests, sales to U.S. bookstores and wholesalers, or to inquire about quantity discounts, please contact the publisher at the email address above.

Printed in the United States of America

Library of Congress Control Number: 2016914055

ISBN 978-0-9968060-3-9

10 9 8 7 6 5 4 3 2

CONTENTS

PART 1
An Idea 1
Program 4
Bob Jackson 10
Loans for Ewert-Rucker House 11
Angry Neighbor 12
Participants 14
Heckendorf 15
Gordon Ewert 17
Excavation 18
Reinforcing and Pouring 19
Steel 22
Walking the Beams 23
Parents Visit 26
From Mother's Diary 28
Wood Framing 29
Symptom 31
Gordon's Operation 32
The House 35
Broaching the Subject 38
Dropping the Subject 39
Selling the Amalfi House 40
Building Department 41
Pepsi Commercial 42
Theme 44
House Move 45
Interior Arrangements 47
Space Ship 48
While Surfing 49
Christmas 50
Living 51
Personal Resources Drained 53
How We Lived 54
Living in the House 55

CONTENTS (continued)

The Pedestal House 57
Money 59
Karon 61
Funeral 63
Dick Haines 64
Possible Teaching Profession 65
Yard Work 69
Tool Space 70
Home Life 70
Bedtime Stories 72
Baby Sitters 74
Drinking 74
Photos of Pedestal House 75
Adamson Commission 77
Comments 80
Advent of Money 81
Context 82
Home Section 83
Singing 90
Evening Outlook 91
Tour Preparation 93
Home Tour 95
Nine Days Rain 97
After the Home Tour 100
Building News 101
Children's Life 103
Hal Rosson 104
Wine and Flu 106
Running 107
Thoughts on Moving 109
September 24, 1970 110

CONTENTS (continued)

PART 2
- Fire 115
- Death of a House 116
- Yellins' 125
- Mrs. Mudd 131
- Linc's Letter 133
- Fire Pictures 136
- Maison De Ville 139
- Evening Outlook Article 142
- Scanning Malibu 145
- New Office 147
- Family Life 152
- Parent's Visit 156
- Feelings About the Year 157
- The I. R. S. 159
- Life Savers 160
- Lew Dominy 160
- Steve Wooley 162
- Richard Sol 162
- Toby Watson 163
- Why OK to Build 164
- Resnicks 166
- The Design 166
- Coming to Terms 168
- Malibu Times Article 171
- Oval Medallion 171
- Rucker House Number 2 172
- Working on the Job 173
- Birth of a House 182
- Condominium Move 185

CONTENTS (continued)

New House 196
Resuming Life 198
Running 201
Office Life 201
Los Angeles Times 202
Publication 203
Sol and Another Home Tour 211
Final Salute 212

A LITTLE BIT OF FOREWORD

Born just outside of Chicago, I attended the University of Illinois in Champaign-Urbana graduating with Bachelor of Science in architecture. I then worked as a draftsman in Denver, San Diego, and Pasadena where I got married to Karon Conan and in the same year received my California license to practice architecture. I continued drafting in Glendale and after three years became chief designer of contemporary houses in Brentwood, California. I then teamed with two contractors and built two houses for sale in Santa Monica Canyon, and when after the first year the first one came up for sale, Karon and I moved into our first home. Over the next few years Karon had three beautiful daughters and I went into business for myself with a partner for a year in Pacific Palisades. When it wasn't working, we dissolved our partnership and I opened my own office on the beach just east of the Malibu pier. The next few years I worked designing mid-century houses mostly in Malibu and Santa Barbara and in 1954 I finished an eight-unit apartment building in Santa Monica for my client and friend, Gordon Ewert. That's where the story of *Trial by Fire* begins. Gordon and I inspired each other to do a modern, mid-century house in Malibu to sell for profit. We'd continue building houses for sale as a side business for fun and profit. Gordon would be the hands-on contractor and I the hands-on architect. In good faith we began our adventure.   Doug

Trial By Fire
A Tale of Two Houses

PART 1
PEDESTAL HOUSE

AN IDEA

Gordon Ewert was delighted with the experience of building a beautiful eight-unit apartment I had designed for him. The publication that came out a year after completion convinced him he wanted to try again. He invited me to an early breakfast and we had the first of many discussions about how we were both going to make it big in the building business; Doug Rucker, Architect, Gordon Ewert, Builder. Gordon was 41, I was 36 and both of us were strongly into our career-building phase, but we had more enthusiasm than money. Gordon's dream, soon to be mine, was to find a lot and build a house for sale. With the profit we'd invest in a similar adventure. We wouldn't build an ordinary house, but one of outstanding contemporary design; a piece of architecture of which we could both be proud. Having had too much coffee, we responded enthusiastically to each other and within a few weeks of determined looking and contacting real estate agents we found a seller, Gus Konz, a commercial flyer and part time real estate agent. I've always thought of Gus as *The Father of the Pedestal House.*

Gus lived with his wife at the end of a cul-de-sac on Harbor Vista Drive in the former Shafer house, the home I'd helped contractor, Nick Schiro, remodel a few years back. Gus Konz, between cross-country flights as an American Airlines Captain, worked as a part time Malibu real estate agent for Louis Busch. He'd been flying commercial jet-craft to Japan, the South Pacific and Australia, but for the past several years had a steady route between Los Angeles and New York. As a real estate agent, Gus was familiar with architects in the area, particularly me, since I had previously worked on his own home and was practically the only architect in Malibu at that time. He'd seen my work and believed I was a responsible architect. He liked the idea of being a key part of what appeared to be a forthright team. He saw us as bringing into existence something creative and beautiful while paying him for what he thought was a useless and undevelopable property.

Gus agreed to sell us the 2/3rd acre site with a 400-foot driveway easement for $8,500.00. Terms would be as follows: Nothing down, five percent interest paid yearly with nothing due on the principle for three years and a subordination clause to a construction loan. A subordination clause is an agreement stating the seller is willing to accept a second trust deed. A second trust deed allows the lending institution to hold the first trust deed; mandatory when obtaining a building loan. In case of default the institution holding a first trust deed will be paid first. The owner of the second trust deed would be paid second with remaining funds.

Things were working nicely. We had no money invested, but did have a piece of property on which we could get a loan, build, sell, and later pay off the second trust deed. If there were anything left, we'd split the profits and start the next project. Gus Konz was our miracle man, our *Sugar Daddy*, how could we *not* build our first dream house?

With great courage and after many discussions with my wife, Karon, Gordon and I signed the papers causing whatever adventure was to happen, to happen next. During weekdays we tramped 400 feet down the dangerously steep driveway to the beginning of our precipitous property and admired the view. The driveway easement, graded a couple of years ago from a few bulldozer passes, was covered with sage, mustard weed, monkey flower and

A Tale of Two Houses

an occasional sumac. In a narrow, uncomfortably paved slope, the passage began from the Harbor Vista Drive cul-de-sac and sloped gently downward toward the ocean. It then turned 90 degrees to the left and dropped steeply at 33 percent for a hundred and fifty feet before doing an almost U-turn to the right and again dropping steeply at 24 percent, then left again to end abruptly at the beginning of our sloping property. Passage was hazardous, but once the site was reached, it was close to the center of Malibu with a magnificent view.

The buildable portion of the property was about ninety feet wide by sixty feet deep on a 3:1 downslope. It was far from ideal because its only access was through an impossibly steep and narrow driveway. There was no flat spot to put the house, nor could we imagine how one could be created. The view and the price were what sold us. The semi-buildable site was on a slim promontory 125 feet above the center of Malibu overlooking Surfrider Beach with an overwhelming view of ocean, canyon and mountains. As far as the eye could see the ocean spread from east to west. To the east was Palos Verde's peninsula. Off Palos Verdes peninsula, Catalina floated in a haze like a dream. At twilight, the curving lights of Santa Monica shown like a rim of sparkling jewels. Smoke billowed from the stacks of the Hyperion Treatment Plant leaving trails of white steam drifting inland. Rising or descending 747's at LAX twinkled at night like slow moving fireflies. In the early morning seventy-five miles away and jutting surprisingly from the horizon, was the conical shape of Mount San Jacinto that sprang into existence like a newly born Mount Fuji. Directly below our building site, the flat, alluvial land was packed with the colorful energy of twenty-three acres of blooming geraniums. They spread in long lines and rectangles of purple, red and white lighting up the landscape in daytime and glowing mysteriously at night. A mountain range, plunging 3,000 feet from Piuma Road to the ocean skirted the easterly side of Malibu Creek that flowed gently toward the ocean. During heavy rainstorms, Malibu Creek roared between willows and sun-bleached boulders to the Pacific where it slipped under the bridge to the lagoon and was filtered through mounds of beach sand, or sometimes moved languorously along winding, narrow channels to the sea. Surfrider Beach stretched from Malibu Pier on the east to the Malibu Movie Colony on the west and continued along the unimposing beach houses that defined the *"Old Road." (Malibu Road.)*

PROGRAM

With the lot tied up, Gordon and I had a meeting in my office and I began to interview him like he was a new client. I found him unresponsive. I said, *"Gordon, what kind of house are we going to build?"*
　"I don't know. Probably a three bedroom, two and one-half baths, with a provision to grow."
　"What should the house look like?"
　"It's up to you. I've always been partial to something Japanese. Perhaps an American post-and-beam house with Japanese overtones."
　My mentor had been Kenneth M. Nishimoto who was born in Japan and was presently one of the members of the American Institute of Architects leading annual architectural tours to Japan. Educated at USC, Ken's methods were not very different than those of my peers, Gordon Drake, Pierre Koenig, Richard Neutra, Raphael Soriano, Quincy Jones, Craig Ellwood, and others. All were significant *50's* architects and all were in the modern architectural history of Southern California. They had built homes derived from, and in some part influenced by the simple wood designs and joinery of the Japanese. I was among friends. I felt at home.
　I thought Gordon would want to express his opinion about the design of a house. After all it was half his. I

expected him to be looking over my shoulder, guiding and supervising and changing my efforts. None of that was to happen. Gordon had been a Marine on Southern Pacific islands like Saipan, Guadal-Canal, Iwo-Jima, Corregidor and others. He was a sniper who'd been on too many missions and had shot too many enemies. He told me he'd learned at least one thing in the service: *"Seize your desire while you have it and follow your guts. Show no hesitation in doing exactly what your heart tells you to do. Astound the world with your uniqueness. Life is too short to waste on anything discomforting or boring. We should not work just to make money. I've seen too many young people die never having completed longed-for adventures."* Gordon was convinced of his philosophy. He was to do only that kind of creative work that absorbed him. His philosophy was the power behind his unflinching way of life. I had to agree.

This was new information for me. I'd not been in the service. With the exception off Don Patton and a few of my college buddies, I'd met very few surviving warriors from the theaters of either Europe or the South Pacific. I was disturbed by the thought of Gordon's life. In his place, I wondered how I would have reacted in a war of such brutality and immorality. Obviously his superior physical ability and intelligence had enabled him to survive where others had not. I had never thought of life and death in the same terms that Gordon had been forced to think. This serious unpleasantness caused wakeful nights. Gordon was producing a life-change in me. Here was a mature man who'd been through a ghastly war and whose expertise was killing humans. I couldn't believe it. Did he have a gun? Would he kill again? Would he become crazy, lose it, kill me? In the war he was considered a hero. Privately he could not forgive himself for heinous acts he was forced to commit under threat of his own death. Gordon was pleased to leave me alone to design our house *by myself*.

While my draftsman, Bill was working on other things,

or I was alone after work, or early in the morning before work, or during time between office phone calls, I'd spend time sketching. My thoughts were filled with Gordon's ideas. He was right. I should spend time on what *I* wanted to do. I was internalizing his philosophy. Life was short. Gordon was leaving me alone and giving me permission to put my heart in my work; to show the world my view. I was to prove to my contemporaries and myself what *I* was like. An architect's work is expressive of what the architect is! I would be me! This was *my* house. My first! The house would have no limiting budget and no other input but my own. For this one time I was going to do a house *I* liked! The house would be my heart. My heart would be the house. I was in love with post-and-beam work. I had an affinity for Japanese methods. My only limitations would be my talent. Karon was pregnant and not bothering me. She'd already agreed Gordon and I were involved in a speculative adventure. She hoped it would end in more money. The house was not to be her house. I was free of her input. What was I waiting for?

Since the buildable area was so small it seemed the only way I could get a house on the property was to provide parking at the beginning of a dividing line between the driveway easement and our steep lot. Afterward, I'd provide a motor court so cars could park, turn around, and get back up the hill. There was barely enough room for an entry. That settled, the only remaining place for the house was above the motor court, but since the floor of the motor court was five to fifteen feet above the ground, the area under the motor court area would be extensive. To design the house *below* the motor court, I'd only have room for windows on two sides, the other two being buried under the turn-around space. If, on the other hand, I put the house at least eight feet above the court, I could have windows and decks on all four sides. To do this, I'd have to support the house on a 25-foot square pedestal reaching to the upper floor, a maximum of 35 feet above the ground. Half the house would be cantilevered into space and the other half cantilevered over the motor court doubling as a covered space for cars.

I sketched the motor court floor with entry and bath. Above, to distribute the weight evenly, it was advisable I *balance* the house on a pedestal. The upper floor would be 45-feet square, symmetrically placed over a pedestal 25-feet square. How to get up there? The answer would be in the geometric center of the pedestal, a circular stairway eight feet in diameter. Aha! Why not peak the roof over the stairway with a skylight?

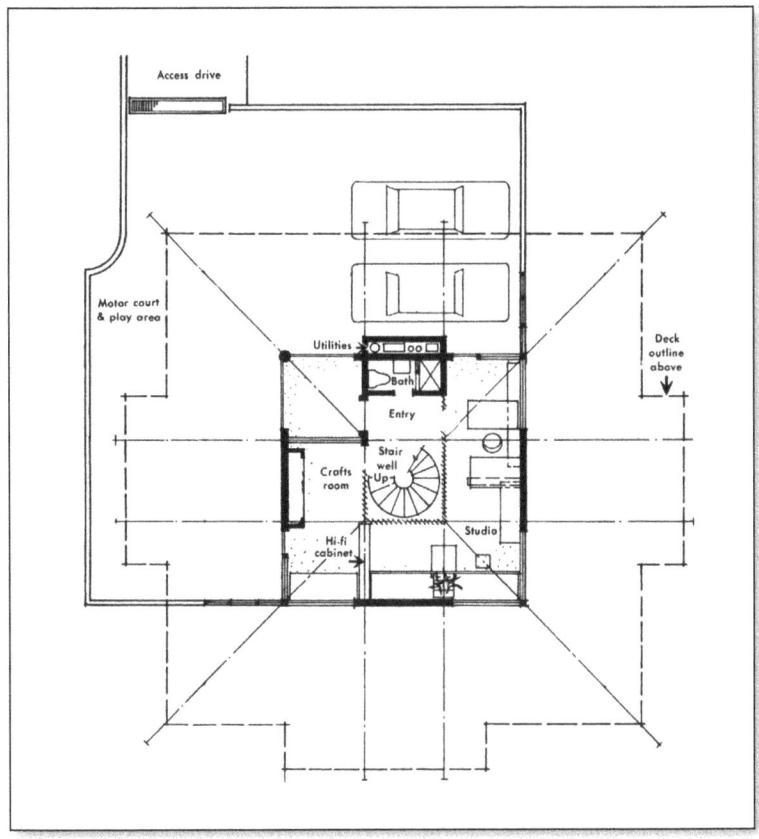

1. *Pen sketch of pedestal house – lower floor plan.*

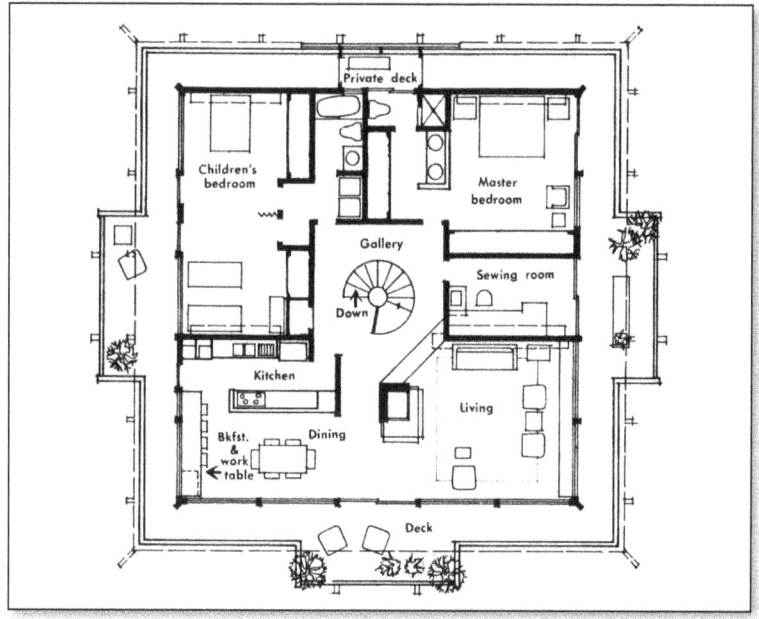

2. Pen sketch of pedestal house - upper floor plan.

This would light an interior art gallery and walkway around the circular stairs to all the rooms - a sort of atrium. I was living it up! Expressing myself was fun! I didn't have to argue or convince. If I didn't like something I'd erase it and do it over. I'd get it the way I liked.

When the design was largely finished, my state of euphoria was weakening and my conception looked back at me. It was staring me back to such an extent that my face flushed and I became embarrassed. I felt as I had after painting the mural on my apartment wall ten-years earlier; a work done with more passion than talent, more uncontrolled desire than reason, a work done with heart and negligible mind. During my objective moments, when the mural was almost finished I'd become painfully aware I'd shown more of my inner self than intended. Artwork expresses the artist. Architectural work expresses the architect. If artist and architect are neurotic, then neurosis has to show. *(Question:*

How do I keep my inner conflicts from showing in my public work?)

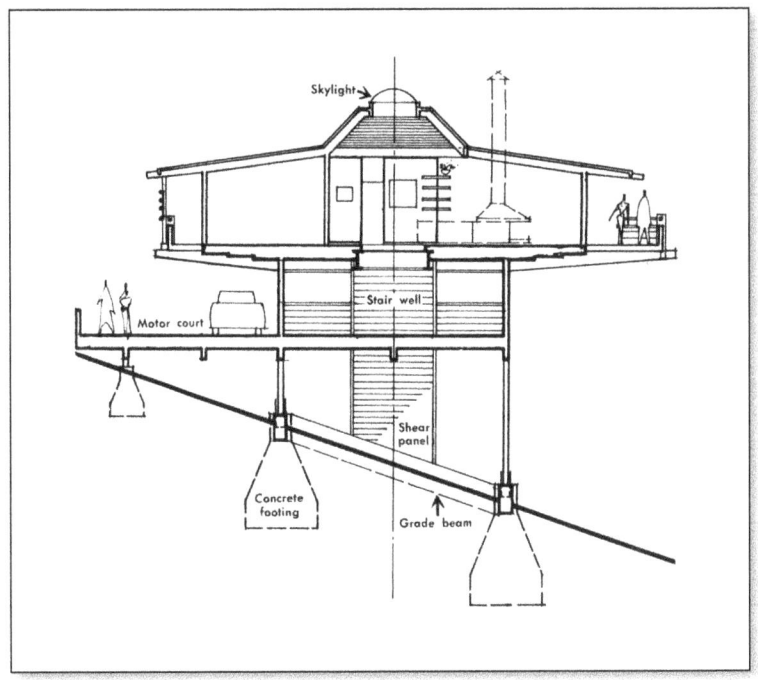

3. Pen sketch off pedestal house – section.

At times like these, I'd look to Gordon to change things, to make rules, to express discontent, to moderate my full expression, to frown and be mildly dissatisfied. I wanted him to be my client, force a budget, express limitations, and agree it would be nice *if* we could afford it. But Gordon liked the design. He wouldn't rationalize the cost or my passion. His attitude was to let it all hang out. He said, *"Is this what you want to do?"* I stuttered, "Yes. I don't have any other ideas." When in the movie *Amadeus*, Mozart was asked to change a few notes of his composition he was appalled! He'd created the music perfectly. It had just the right amount of notes. He'd expressed what he wanted to say completely. How dare anyone attempt to change one note? You might as well tell an elm leaf its design is incorrect. Though far from being an architect of the same caliber as Mozart was a musician, the principle was the same.

I'd struck the limit of my talent. In the latter part of 1965, the house was born the only way it could have been born. Beads of perspiration formed on my face. My design made me feel self-conscious. It was daring, expensive, eye-catching, exciting, and a benchmark of some sort. It looked like a flying saucer. I would be considered either a genius or a fool. If the house failed for reasons I couldn't understand, I'd never have another job. If considered a work of a genius, I'd have more of the same to build. I was young and in the career building stage. The pluses outweighed the minuses. It would be difficult to get a loan on such a different house. Gordon liked the design. It belonged to both of us. I threw reason to the wind and let the unconscious mind decide: *GO!*

BOB JACKSON

Through my business in architecture I came to know and like Bob Jackson, a busy professional delineator of architectural projects and a superb fine-artist. He worked in his private studio on a bluff overlooking Malibu Cove Colony and houses on the shoreline of Escondido Beach. Bob had been an alcoholic, but also in the program and alcohol-free for over ten years.

Bob saw my designs and in discovering I had something unusual to say for Malibu, generously offered to do a free rendering of my house. The rendering allowed me to clearly show our intentions to friends, relatives, colleagues, and most importantly to the bank. It was highly useful in advertising and public relations and a gesture by Bob for which I shall always feel grateful.

4. *Rendering of the pedestal house. Bob Jackson's gift.*

LOANS FOR EWERT-RUCKER HOUSE

In January of 1965 Rick Davidson, my long time architect friend was assisting me doing drafting work in his free time and had just finished the pedestal house drawings. Our next job was to get a building permit. That happened in due time while we shopped for a construction loan. With the help of my carpenter friends, Heckendorf and Diefenderfer, Gordon estimated the cost of the house at $80,000.00. In 1965 lending continued to remain easier, but getting a loan on such a radically conceived house would be difficult. Harry would assume the responsibility of the construction work. Gordon would remain half-owner but chief builder. When not working on the job he'd be keeping books and furnishing building materials for Harry and John.

Contacting lending agencies took several months. On our list were Bank of America, Santa Monica Bank, American and California Federal Savings and Loan, and three or four others. After being denied by the rest of the institutions, Glendale Federal Savings & Loan was the only one *remotely* interested in lending on such a steep site with such a different looking project. Other agencies were used to lending on standard plaster and nail-on-window houses on which they could do reliable comparables, but they were reluctant to invest in anything so out-of-the-ordinary as a mid-century post-and-beam house on a pedestal. To them it was something from outer space. In case the borrower defaults, lenders are required to have a fallback position. Under a default, if the mortgage goes unpaid, to recover their investment they'd have to foreclose and sell the house. If the house wouldn't sell at market value they'd have to dump it below the loan amount and try to write off their loss. Standard lending institutions weren't going to risk savers money by investing in unproven, non-standard houses.

ANGRY NEIGHBOR

Our 2/3rd acre lot had been split from a larger piece. A slim driveway easement, about 400 feet long, began at the cul-de-sac and sloped down a narrow driveway between two houses. It looped down and away and around an almost U-turn, then dipped diagonally back to the property line before descending steeply to our site. Our neighbors, the owner's of the house who'd bought their property with the easement *already granted*, were angry that Gordon and I, or indeed anyone, would want to build below on that tiny, steep, impossible slope. They were unhappy someone would be utilizing the narrow easement located not more than five feet away from their house. Ascending traffic would disturb them grinding up the hill. Headlights would shine in their windows and disrupt privacy. In their minds, I assume they visualized an ugly, white, blob on the site below with lights at night disturbing their tranquil evenings. Any house would compromise what they considered their unadulterated view, but especially a weird one. It was not plausible that any of their view would have been obstructed. Our house would be fifty or more feet below their house and didn't interrupt the horizon line nor would it blot but a fraction of the geranium gardens. Like most of us, they had difficulty with change and yearned for the status quo. Peeking through their bushes from their little window to our descending driveway the disturbed wife was especially incensed with representatives of lending institutions making inspections. Up and down the hill possible lenders walked and slid in leather-soled shoes, ties and fancy clothes. The building inspector's visit's lent reality to her greatest fear - *the project was going ahead!*

At 9:00 AM one morning in what Gordon and I thought was our final opportunity to get money, I met a field officer from Glendale Federal Savings & Loan on our street not too close to our angry neighbor's house. Under Jim's *(not his real name)* arm was a rolled set of our plans. We'd just returned from walking and slipping down the precipitous overgrown grade to inspect the even steeper site. I'd have to classify it a zero in his mind as an agreeable place to build a house, but the panorama was nothing short of overwhelming. The design took wonderful advantage of all the views. During our discussion Jim looked uncertain. His thinking involved the difficulty of building on a steep site with such an uncompromising access. I'd guess he was about 60/40 against lending. Materials would have to be carried by hand. Concrete trucks couldn't make it up or down the grade. Access to the site was extremely difficult. He wanted to make a loan for his company, but was unsure of Gordon as a new builder-contractor. He was questioning our ability to finish construction within the budget and if the house didn't sell, would we be able to make the payments? Projecting a sure *no*, Jim, doubtful in his suit and tie, looked exactly like the lending official he was and I probably looked pleading and desperate in Levi's, work shoes and T-shirt.

At nine-thirty Mrs. Smith, *(not her real name)* in curlers, housecoat, and worn slippers, marched out of her house and with hands on hips stood defiantly in front of us and demanded, *"Well?! What are you up to now?!"*

Since I always treated people politely, I quietly replied, *"I'm seeing about a loan for a house."* She said she didn't like it! The property was too steep! The traffic and noise would disrupt her family! The neighborhood didn't want a house down there! Building on that steep site was insane and ridiculous!

Three people were standing alone in the middle of the street near the cul-de-sac. A belligerent woman, head thrust forward in confrontational pose, a questioning architect in jeans and T-shirt, and a well-dressed banker in a fresh suit-jacket attempting to grasp what was happening.

"Jim, here, is going to lend me the money." I said.

Mrs. Smith glowered at Jim and demanded, *"Well, are you?"*

Jim ever so slightly rocked on his heels while the question hung in the air. Jim felt more or less insulted with the unanticipated rudeness of the women in curlers. He disliked the self-absorption of my angry neighbor. Then, after hesitating a moment, he looked her in the eye and said softly and convincingly, *"Yes!"*

If Mrs. Smith had not been so disagreeable, chances were six-to-four Jim would've answered, *"No."* I got the loan because our neighbor had ticked off Jim. The Lord works in mysterious ways.

PARTICIPANTS

I was a man in context. I had a wife and three kids, one, three and five, living in my self-designed house on Amalfi Drive with a self-designed rent-free office on the beach near the Malibu pier. I was looking forward to building a smashing house for speculation overlooking Surfrider Beach, the Serra Retreat, Malibu Creek, Catalina, the Movie Colony, and some of the most beautiful scenery in one of the world's most coveted areas.

At 36, I was six years into my Malibu practice and

continuing a career within the context of the community. My immediate concern was whatever was in front of me. It seemed I had too many responsibilities, bills to pay, family to maintain and clients to serve.

The World News described the horrors of the world and rarely its wonders. It particularly described our Vietnam War. A good portion of the country vehemently objected to our involvement. Fighting in Vietnam was irrational and everyone in America was depressed and disheartened. Our country seemed never to awaken to a feeling of peace. In spite of negative feelings about an unjust war, my job was to support my family and pursue my work to the best of my ability.

HECKENDORF

In my former jobs I'd been relying on Harry Heckendorf with his carpenter helper John Diefenderfer and recommended them to Gordon to help us build our Malibu *"spec"* house. Harry was a close friend of my former landlord, Louis Busch, one of Malibu's first and most reliable Real Estate Firms. Louis' father had worked with Real Estate Agent, Dave Diefenderfer in selling the first available Malibu parcels for the then owner, May K. Rindge. Dave Diefenderfer, John Diefenderfer's uncle, was a medium-sized elderly man with white hair who smoked a pipe. John Diefenderfer also smoked a pipe while he worked with Harry. When I suggested to a new owner that Heckendorf and Diefenderfer might build their home, the owner's eyebrows rose slightly before their faces broke into a grin. Heckendorf and Diefenderfer? The combination of names was odd, but their work was not. Harry built the Zenn house, my first in Malibu and most recently for Gerry and Ellie Hauffe who were thrilled with Heckendorf & Deifenderfer's work.

5. Doug and Harry Heckendorf.

Harry was not a licensed contractor, but a carpenter who worked on the job and acted as the owner's agent to facilitate its completion. For ordering materials, hiring subcontractors, doing general supervision, keeping books, and coordinating the work, his charges were slightly higher than an average carpenter's wages. But his cost for the whole job was always less than a licensed general contractor's because he didn't charge the contractors usual profit of 10% for labor and 10% for overhead. He charged the wholesale cost of labor and materials plus a necessary amount for insurance and workman's compensation.

    I liked Harry and John because they liked to work and while on the job were tireless and enthusiastic. Harry had been raised in Nebraska on a farm and told us he was out in the field an hour before sun-up and worked until an hour after sundown. He said we'd never *believe* how hard life was in Nebraska. Harry brought the same unwavering energy to California. He owned his own house and was married with two children. He'd put in an hour of work on his vegetable garden before coming to our job and a full days' work as a carpenter-contractor, then go to his other job maintaining an apartment building he owned in Santa Monica. There was no stopping Harry. He knew no other way to live. I suspect the reason was having been brought up on the hard plains of Nebraska.

GORDON EWERT

Among his other proficiencies Gordon was also a fine carpenter. He was motivated to do things correctly. His work and his heart were on the same page. We agreed he would be the chief on our Malibu *"spec"* job. Gordon was delighted with Harry Heckendorf and John Diefenderfer and treated them as partners. Gordon's job was to keep the books, organize the work of the subcontractors and make sure the materials were on the job and ready for installation. When that was done he'd assist as a carpenter.

About five-foot-ten, lean and strong, he had the appearance of a formidable blond college halfback. Joining the Marines at seventeen Gordon was trained as a sniper. Within a year he was active in the South Pacific participating in some of histories most difficult and deadly invasions. Gordon's natural brilliance, so I'm told, was tempered with a strong conscience and a deep sense of duty. He was an excellent military man and his fellow Marines knew him as a man of quickness, intelligence and superior physical ability.

My association with Marine Corps sniper, Gordon, was maturing. His stories acquainted me with the intolerable, immoral, and deadly conditions of war. Strangely, twenty years after fighting and killing the Japanese for four long years, Gordon's hobby was growing Japanese Bonsai trees. I saw the results of his Bonsai labor when I visited him in his tiny Malibu house perched on a bluff overlooking the ocean and Pacific Coast Highway.

Gordon was an excellent skier. I saw films of the world champion downhill racer skiing the slopes in and out of trees, leaping hummocks, jumping from snowy cliffs and landing, balanced and confident thirty yards away. Shots of this champion astounded me, but I was overwhelmed when I learned Gordon was skiing behind him and filming him on the way down. It took a while for that knowledge to sink in. Gordon was not only skiing the same slopes as the champion, but was doing it while taking motion pictures of him with his camera.

Gordon was also a night lobster fisherman. When I asked him one day where he was last night he told me he'd been harvesting lobster from his traps. Gordon would take a skiff out in the ocean about midnight wearing a wet suit, flippers, goggles and helmet with light and dive for lobsters he sold to local restaurants. He was a heroic and surprisingly unusual person.

EXCAVATION

We got geology and soils reports from a Pasadena firm called Converse Engineering and Geology Company. The Geologist and I worked out the foundation structure and a young apprentice of mine, Richard Sol, and I did the working drawings and got the permit. The entire structure would be supported on four *bell-bottomed* caissons at each corner of a twenty-six and a half foot-square foundation. The tops of the caissons would be tied together with twelve-inch by twenty-four-inch deep concrete grade beams with steel reinforcing bars bent vertically into the caisson tops and horizontally into themselves at the corners. Vertical six by six-inch square steel pipe-columns would rise to the second floor at each corner, as did four-inch round steel pipe-columns at eight points. A total of twelve columns would bear the weight of twelve horizontal tapered steel beams at the second floor cantilevering twelve feet in four directions. Four cantilevered tapered steel beams would project diagonally at each corner cantilevering seventeen feet. Total steel columns - twelve. Total steel beams - twelve.

Because of the job's difficulty, the excavation contractor had to think carefully. A better access would be from below through the geranium gardens, but how was he going to get a heavy drill-rig up the steep slope? He decided to bring the drill-rig up by tying chains to a bulldozer and with the engines of both the bulldozer and drill-rig grinding at low gear, hoped to creep up the loosely graded road to the site.

In drilling *bell-bottomed-caissons* the rig would drill a three-foot diameter hole to whatever depth was required, in this case about twelve feet deep. Then the operator would install successively wider drill bits increasing the diameter as the bell deepened and widened. Eventually the bottom slowly belled into the proper shape, hence, the name *bell-bottomed-caissons*. Today bell-bottomed caissons are rarely used in favor of *friction piers* that derive their support from the friction created between the soil and concrete on the *vertical sides* of the concrete column. On the other hand, bell-bottoms derive support by bearing directly on the soil below.

One day Gordon and I got on a ladder and climbed down the bell-bottomed caissons for a look. Sitting on the floor at the bottom of the caisson we were astounded and I might say thrilled looking up at the sky through the three-foot cylindrical drill-hole. We talked. We examined the strength of the overhanging earth. We were reasonably cautious and slightly uneasy about being down in an empty pit. We comforted ourselves knowing laborers had recently been down the hole for cleaning and they weren't buried. We joked the *belled caisson* was large enough for five guys to sit in a circle at the bottom and play poker. Convinced the bell would support the loads, we thought it a more than suitable solution.

REINFORCING AND POURING

*B*ell-bottom caissons required reinforcing. Gordon had a load of steel bars delivered to the site and Harry and John tied them in place according to the plans. In each of the bottoms of the bells, bars were placed horizontally in a crosshatched pattern supported on slim concrete blocks six inches above the horizontal undisturbed soil. The vertical reinforcing for each of the four caissons was made of twelve steel bars in a hexagonal pattern and tied every couple of feet with 1/2-inch round bars. Vertical reinforcing extended from the bottom of the caisson to six feet above grade. At the top the extensions were later to be bent at ninety degrees horizontally to fit into future grade beams for an indestructible connection.

Again, pouring the concrete would be made from below. When the caisson steel was properly placed, concrete trucks usually holding ten cubic yards were filled only to seven. If completely filled, they would spill when ascending the steep grade. Once the trucks reached the top of the hill the tops of the caissons were still twenty-five feet higher. It was necessary to pump concrete from the lower trucks up the twenty-five feet to the tops of the caissons. On the lower shelf, trucks noisily whirled their drums to mix the concrete and dumped it into a narrow shoot where it flowed to a separate concrete pumping device. The pump then made more whirring noises while concrete was being forced upward through a five-inch diameter hose to the top of the caissons. Strong workmen wrestled the end of the hose aimed down the hole where concrete shot and plopped out the end.

The arrival of trucks supplying concrete were timed to follow one another exactly, so delivery, pumping and distribution came consecutively and on time. For the average caisson to be filled took about fifteen cubic yards of concrete or about two truckloads. When caissons were topped off level to the ground, all that remained were four three-foot round messy slabs of concrete, level with the earth, with six feet of reinforcing steel sticking out the top and bent over to the ground.

At day's end, the sun sinking quietly into a purplish ocean, Gordon and I sat above on the dirt and observed what we'd done. Except for four flat blobs of concrete topped off level with the ground, the site was strikingly empty! We had committed ourselves to paying back thousands of dollars for the cost of plans, geology, permits, structural engineering, excavation, reinforcing steel, and concrete, and the site still looked the same!

Despite the vacant appearance of the site, we'd nevertheless made a strong beginning. The following week a small truck with a trenching device scooped out narrow ditches for grade beams. The twelve-inch by twenty-four-inch deep grade beams took the form of a large square with the four corners connecting the four caisson tops. Bent-over vertical steel from the caissons was already in place and ready to be tied into the grade beams.

(A grade beam is like a standard concrete footing, but is wider and deeper and better reinforced. It is designed to span between two points, (in this case, caisson top to caisson top) without deriving support from the soil beneath.)

The following day Harry and John began building wooden forms for the grade beams and when they were plumb, true and braced, they set the reinforcing steel, installed base plates, and tied foundation bolts to the forms. The grade beams were ready for pouring. The next morning at 7:00 AM ten-yard trucks, short-loaded so as not to spill, growled noisily up the slope and dumped their loads into the concrete pumping device. The wet mix was again forced through the thick hose to a strong man at the outlet and cement rushed like thick mud from the nozzle, slopping, slurping and splattering into place and filling the forms. The long rectangular boxes were quickly filled and laborers standing just outside the forms prodded the wet concrete shoving the ends of two by fours time and again into the mix to remove air bubbles. When they were not prodding they used shovels to move and redistribute the concrete, pulling it along to fill low spots and occasionally throwing shovels-full into neglected places.

Early the following morning the forms were stripped leaving the raw concrete to cure in the open air. After the caissons and grade beams were finished a concrete block man built low foundation walls to hold the motor court framing. Within a couple of weeks the foundation was completed.

In the evening when everybody had left the job and I was alone, the foundations spoke to me of things to come. When foundations are in full view with column plates securely cemented into place, the foundation bolts and hold-downs projecting and ready for attachment, the raw concrete protruding quietly and powerfully a foot or two out of the ground, again I think of the job as being pregnant. When foundations are finished and blatantly exposed for all to see, the die is cast! A suggestion of everything that is to follow is dictated by the foundation. The foundation is the *word*. The foundation is the *thing*. The foundation is nothing less than the base-chord against which is played a beautiful melody.

A joke: After completing the Tower of Pisa the architect says to his friend, *"I skimped a little on the foundations, but nobody will ever know."*

Foundations are fundamental. That means they are essential, basic and crucial. When the foundation has been completed a *key* part has been built.

STEEL

The huge, dark, oily looking six-wheel truck with a load of tapered steel beams chained to the flat bed laboriously turned around in the geranium fields below and backed slowly up the hill. It was standard thinking for an experienced truck driver to *back* the ungainly truck up the hill rather than drive up facing forward. Truck power is stronger in reverse and since it was impossible to turn the truck around on the small pad above, the driver had to choose beforehand his method of return. To lose one's brakes *backing* down the hill was infinitely more dangerous than losing brakes driving forward down the hill.

A Tale of Two Houses

Steel fabricators seem to live in their own world. Where subcontractors like carpenters, cabinet men, plumbers, electricians, roofers, glazers, and so forth, call each other by first names and join each other at the snack truck for jokes and pie, steel men seem to isolate themselves into a small private community. I see steel men as satisfied workmen bringing oily tools, welding equipment, tractors, crane, pulleys, hammers, bolts, rivets, come-alongs, and doing their highly specialized work as a team with vigor and clarity. When our fabricators came they did so with camaraderie, humor, effort, strength, expertise and, as with all professionals, *the structure rose quietly above them.* In the pedestal house, when I say the steel *rose quietly above them*, I mean the cantilevered structure *rose* in some places to a height of thirty-five feet.

6. *View of steel just finished.*

WALKING THE BEAMS

At the southeast corner a horizontal, tapered steel beam pointed directly toward the Palos Verdes Peninsula. At its point the ground was thirty-five feet below. Thereafter the ground sloped steeply a hundred or more feet to the flat alluvial, geranium covered plane formed over millions of years by Malibu Creek.

Now I'm not a steel man, but I've seen pictures of steel workers calmly walking upright along the tops of steel beams perhaps fifty or sixty stories above the miniscule roofs of Chicago or New York City. I was impressed! How could they be so casual? A missed step and they'd fall to a screaming death. Seeing a steel worker atop a super-structure is like plummeting Niagara Falls in a barrel, or bungee jumping the Golden Gate, or flying below the rim of the Grand Canyon. Nevertheless, whether scary but fun, I wanted to walk my own beams.

7. Steel finished and motor court framing begun.

Visiting the job alone one Saturday morning, I gathered my courage and climbed a ladder from the motor court level to the top of the cantilevered structure. Giving up actually walking the beams, I sat down with my feet on either side of the lower flange straddling the highest one thrusting boldly toward Palos Verdes. I grabbed the top flange with my fingers, or should I say knuckles that were certainly white, and inched my way forward moving out on the farthest most protruding beam. Unfortunately, as you may remember, though the beam-tops were level, the beam bottoms tapered upward. Beginning at twenty-four inches deep, at the end they were only eight inches deep

8. Steel framing from below.

As I approached the end I could no longer brace myself as solidly with my feet. I was tippy. Half way out with nothing under me, but thrilling spasms, shivers, and death, I decided to stop. At thirty-five feet above the earth, though it looked a hundred and thirty-five, the view was outstanding and good enough. There was nothing out there but the horizon, a vast expanse of ocean, Palos Verdes, tousled hair and white knuckles. I didn't feel so badly about stopping half way out. After all, I wasn't a steel worker.

As I remember, we started building the pedestal house at the end of 1965, so by the time the foundations and steel substructure were in place, it must have been about March of 1966 when Harry Heckendorf, John Diefenderfer and

Gordon Ewert entered the carpentry phase of construction. Both sides of the exterior walls, including pedestal column and house, were to be clad in horizontal one by eight clear-heart redwood siding. These were the days when clear-heart redwood was not on the endangered list. Both sides of the interior walls were designed in drywall. Gordon, though, had another idea. He had a plastering contractor friend who insisted on giving us a beautiful interior-plastering job at a reasonable price, which he later did in a masterful way.

9. Framing of upper floor

PARENTS VISIT

About this time mother and dad visited from Denver. They were infrequent guests and came to California about once every two years. I had written to them about our building-project-for-sale and had sent them Bob Jackson's rendering. Now I had a chance to show them the idea in person. Someone, probably mother, caught us with a camera at just the right time. It shows dad and I walking down the driveway with me gesturing. It was a lucky and descriptive shot. Dad's reaction was complementary and though he never said so, I felt he was very proud. Dad couldn't often verbally express what he felt. I inferred he liked my new adventure, but it was probably an activity with which he had nothing to compare. Mother was also enthused about the new house and the abilities of her beloved son. She bragged extensively about my work.

10. Beginning of floor framing. I point, dad looks on.

11. Motor court and second floor platform laid out.

12. Doug sorting lumber.

FROM MOTHER'S DIARY

"...all the family had a bite of lunch before we piled into our car for a trip to see Doug's fabulous new home site in Malibu.
  His house is under construction and is up to the floor beams. The view is just unbelievable! The place is half way

up a mountainside overlooking acres of geranium beds all in full bloom and with a wide expanse of ocean beyond. The house is most dramatic according to the large rendering in color and most scary from a financial standpoint. He has taken a large loan and I only hope he can repay it. But the whole thing is exciting and marvelous. He promised us a picture of the rendering.
Sincerely, Evelyn.

WOOD FRAMING

13. House beginning framing stage.

Instead of driving through the geranium gardens below, lumber deliveries were unloaded from big trucks at the top of the driveway, then loaded on to Harry's pick-up truck to be transported by many trips down the driveway to the motor court. Whether drill rigs, concrete, steel or lumber, getting materials to the site was difficult and added time and financial loss to the job.

14. Roof beams installed.

Harry was in charge of the construction and scheduled the work. He and his steady helper, John, put the wood and material in place. When not helping with carpentry, Gordon chased after materials. All construction jobs need what is called a *gopher. Gopher's* keep the work moving at a continuous pace. *(Gopher: means go-for. A person goes for materials.)* Things progressed swiftly and I left my studio often to check the job. It was exciting! I was always astounded by the flowering geraniums, magnificent views of Surfrider Beach, Palos Verdes, Catalina, Malibu Creek, Malibu Colony, and the Serra Retreat. Workers were cooled when the westerly on-shore breezes came up in the afternoon. Shafts of sunlight penetrated the clouds on rainy days creating a mysterious, changing water-tableau on the ocean. Even without the joy of seeing my own design under construction, any trip to the site was stirring.

When the plywood floor was nailed down it created a giant 42-foot square platform with a stairway-hole in the center. The plywood floor could have been a landing pad for a helicopter, or a place to sit in cross-legged contemplation, or a spot for overnight camping, or a place just to just sit and enjoy the view. The flat, square plywood floor as proof of joys to come was by itself optimistic and exciting. But it didn't remain so for long. Harry and John were in process and kept construction moving. Walls were built lying on the floor and then lifted into place, nailed, and braced plumb and true. Roof beams were raised by ladders, pulleys, scaffolding and six sturdy arms. Clip angles and tie-downs were screwed and bolted into place, and there was that special time, as there is on every job, when the structure's reality is first sketched. A time when anyone can see what it will eventually be. It was astounding! It was sensitive! It was decisive! It was strong. It was gentle and a dream coming true. The reality was more than anything I could ever have expected.

Soon a white coat of reflective, fire resistant roofing was floated over several layers of roofing paper and the skylight was installed. Harry and John finished the details of rough construction putting in blocking for the plasterer, nailing final plywood for the shear walls, applying wood siding, and installing decking and handrails. The heating man ran his ducts. The electrician nailed his switch boxes. The glass man roughed in fixed glass and sliding glass doors.

SYMPTOM

One day I got a call from Harry at an odd hour in the evening and I became concerned.

He said, *"There's something strange going on with Gordon. For the last couple of weeks I've been giving him lists of construction material to get at the lumberyard. When he returns he has the wrong items and sometimes forgets major items completely."*

The following week, Harry confronted Gordon. He had returned without another essential piece of material and appeared to be having memory lapses even with clear lists. Gordon had been having serious headaches and apologized profusely. He wondered how he could have forgotten things so simply listed. It was certainly not Gordon's intention to forget materials or not to consult Harry's list. He wondered why this was happening. After an extended period, perhaps two or three weeks, it became unquestionably a symptom that something was not right.

GORDON'S OPERATION

A trip to the Santa Monica Hospital confirmed Gordon had a malignant brain tumor and an immediate operation was necessary. As I knew they would, Harry and John took over the job and while Gordon was having tests, continued construction with no loss of time. After his operation and during recovery, I remember visiting him at the hospital, probably with Tony De Vivo and Gordon's fiancée, Debbie. Gordon was sitting three quarters up by the window with his head in bandages, covers over his chest, and hands relaxed on his lap. He recognized us immediately and appeared cheerful and coherent. For the better part of an hour we sat with him and had a quiet, pleasant conversation.

He said he'd been told the operation had gone well. It had not been painful. He was not put under a complete anesthetic but was partially awake while they removed a large piece of his skull. The pressure and headache pain were instantly relieved; neurosurgeons cut out the cancerous growth and sent him to the recovery room where Gordon quickly regained full wakefulness. For the coming month he was advised to take things easy and rest while doctors monitored his condition. Physical therapy was ordered a few hours a day to help overcome aberrations normally following surgery. While we were there, Gordon's attitude was optimistic and he seemed ready to do whatever was necessary for recovery. He reported the Doctor's *thought they'd got all of it*. Statistics weren't in line with Gordon's optimism however. They showed brain malignancies usually

A Tale of Two Houses

return within a year or so and eventually are fatal.

I was devastated and my heart went out to Gordon. Again, *"There, but for the grace of God, go I!"*

After Gordon was released, his friends, probably Tony De Vivo and Debbie, helped him find someone to stay with him and care for him at his rented house. I would see Gordon every so often during his home confinement. He couldn't read or do the simplest mathematics. I saw his primers. He was studying the alphabet like a first grader and attempting to read child's books. He was also working on the simplest additions.

Nor could he drive. I remember picking Gordon up at his bachelor's house and taking him for a ride in my old MG. Top down and wind gusting, we wound along the serpentine Malibu Canyon Road toward my job in Monte Nido. Gordon sat beside me, hands folded in his lap, hair blowing in the wind and intent on the beauty of the canyon. Speeding past rock walls, turnouts and lookouts, the cliff plunged steeply on the right into Malibu Creek, while on the left it towered to the height of the mountain above. Rounding a curve with a breeze and an electric-blue sky, the brilliance of stratified rock across the creek came suddenly into view. On the opposite canyon wall the outcroppings were ablaze in the setting sun and I heard Gordon faintly whisper, *"So beautiful." (Pause) "So beautiful."*

I thought to myself, *"Gordon is noticing how beautiful life is on earth. He's keenly alert and knows he's leaving."* I said nothing, but knew Gordon was giving the earth a last look before he died.

Did I understand what Gordon was going through? Because of the war and his brain tumor, Gordon's perspective of life was different than mine. I grew up, got a degree, got married, got a license, opened a business, had children, built a house, and would probably retire and die happy. Gordon's life should have been like mine. It was hideously destroyed by the nightmare of war. He was imprinted for life by trying to live four years in a hell of atrocities that were beyond my imagination. No! I didn't understand Gordon!

15. Gordon resting after the operation.

Nor could I imagine myself dying of something so unlikely as a brain tumor. I was unacquainted with brain tumors. Nor could I imagine dying at so young an age as forty-two. After all, I was a naive thirty-six-year-old; still an uninterrupted youth. The young are fearless even when it comes to death. Death at thirty-six or at forty-two never occurred to me. No! I didn't understand dying.

But because I couldn't understand Gordon's war experiences and his imminent death didn't mean I didn't care about him. We had a lot in common. We were both athletic, loved building, and could artistically separate the good from the bad. I cared about Gordon, but even so, my life was radically changed by his illness and approaching death. I didn't ask for this situation. My plans were interrupted too. I had planned to build a spec house with him and then go forward with him to similar adventures. Faced with this predicament, what was I going to do now?

THE HOUSE

After a few weeks in the hospital, Gordon was sent home and for the time being I waited to see what would develop. He seemed sure he'd recover, but I didn't know the Doctor's thinking. I had no reason to believe he wouldn't recover. The building of the pedestal house would lack the benefit of his services though Harry and John could continue quite well without him. Harry would go for materials even though it cut into his carpentry time, but that was customary for Harry.

I was content with this *wait-and-see* attitude for a time, but as the months went by, Gordon made little progress in his healing let alone reading and arithmetic. He was never able to drive again. His severe headaches returned. I'm sure he was taking painkillers of some sort, probably morphine.

After the operation, when Gordon hadn't experienced the rapid recovery he'd hoped for, we had a serious talk. Gordon felt that under the circumstances he couldn't continue in our partnership and that I should build and sell the project on my own. He was evidently too preoccupied with pain, inability to read or calculate and unable to return to his former motivation and enthusiasm. Regarding the purely speculative profit we were supposed to make, he was willing to let that go and agreed to have his name removed from the loan and property agreements. He later signed papers to that affect and suddenly I found I was without a partner in our spec-house project. I learned several months later that his condition had worsened and that he had moved to Santa Monica being nursed by a female empathetic person.

16. *Harbor Vista house almost half constructed.*
(Spring 1966)

In 1966 during the finishing stages of the pedestal house, I found myself locked into a thirty-year mortgage with Glendale Federal and property payments due in a little over two years. Projected building costs showed it impossible *anyone* could have completed the house sufficiently for sale with the eighty thousand borrowed. Fate decreed Gordon die. Fate decreed Karon and I were responsible to pay back our two house loans.

Then it occurred to me I could either sell or buy the spec house! How could that idea *not* enter my head? When the dream-house was finished, the idea of profit was uncertain, not only because we wouldn't have found the money to finish it, but also because of the precipitous driveway and unusual design. I surmised at the time the steep drive and strange house would frighten buyers *and* lenders. Not too many buyers would *like* a strange house. Because of a surplus of lender money the Southern California area had become overbuilt. Building was no longer profitable. The lender's said, *"Money's gone back east. Houses and apartments are over-sold. Foreclosures and sales out of foreclosure are common. It's a buyer's market!"* For me, selling in a *buyer's market* meant reducing the sales price and the probability of accepting an unknown waiting period to sell a strange house on a difficult site while paying back three mortgages. *(One for my Amalfi Drive house, one to Glendale Federal for the spec house, and a third to Gus Konz for the second trust deed.)*

Regarding buying it: There would be certain advantages. I would not profit from my work, but in the long run ownership at such a bargain rate would be better than money. I could move my family and my office into an unfinished house and complete it later. I would not have to pay a real estate commission or a builder's profit. I would have at least two and a half years or so to earn money to pay off our second trust deed. If we sold our Amalfi house after having lived in it for seven years we should make a substantial profit. That profit might help cover overages on the new house. If the Amalfi house were sold, the thirty years new mortgage payments seemed within my budget. Despite the present slowdown in building, on paper, the record showed I made more money with each advancing year. As an architect I was gathering prestige through recent publications. Time on my rent-free office was coming to a close. Working from an office in the new Malibu home meant I would not have to raise money for office rent. If I opted for selling the pedestal house and renting my office space at a minimum of $500.00 a month, the office rent would *exceed* the new mortgage payment on the pedestal house. Financially, it was better to own. I'd save future office rent. The ideal location of the new house would not only be convenient, but the unusual pedestal design for a budding architect should be an eye-catching asset.

The pluses were too great to pass up. I had a brief window of time to act. I was following Gordon's philosophy, *going with my heart, using my mind as a helper.* Acting on the idea would be one of the keys to a perfect life - infusing passion with intelligence. Buying my own pedestal house would mean my dream to live and work in Malibu was coming true!

BROACHING THE SUBJECT

I returned to our Amalfi home with exciting news. *"Karon, what would you think of moving into the new pedestal house?"* Karon was hesitant. We talked. I explained the reasons why. Karon told me she understood my reasoning but she didn't *want* to move from her Santa Monica Canyon home. She'd already made arrangements for Viveka, my eldest daughter, to start first grade in the elementary school at the bottom of the hill. Viveka in fact was excited about school and had already attended a week of classes and was adjusting beautifully. We had a comfortable house in the middle of a good neighborhood with four children as playmates *(the Blacks)* next door and others close by. Karon had given birth to all her children there. We'd been in our house for seven or so years, had improved it, and it was a short walk to our beloved beach. All her friends were nearby. The Amalfi house was close to shopping, theaters, dentists, pediatricians, and her mother and father who lived in Pacific Palisades were handy for baby-sitting. She knew our Amalfi house intimately since she and I had painted every inch of the interior. We'd worked seemingly forever getting a carpet to replace an imported one of grass squares and I'd labored hard building my *(seldom used)* home architectural studio.

We'd suffered through Eric Armstrong's recommendations of installing the fast-growing Wigandia Caracasana along the driveway with its needle-like poisons. What would her friends think? Would her personal friends be willing to travel into the country *(Malibu)* to visit? She was after all, *a city girl.* Malibu was in the country. She'd be a *country girl.* A move to Malibu was a move to a completely different world. Our early marriage adventures had been in the Amalfi house, to which she'd felt herself to be a major contributor. She'd *not* been involved in the pedestal house. Shouldn't a wife be a contributor to her own new home?

DROPPING THE SUBJECT

*B*ecause of Gordon Ewert's withdrawal, Karon *had* to sign the loan papers with Glendale Federal and Gus Konz. She would replace Gordon as my partner in the pedestal house venture whether she liked it or not. This was a severe blow. She would now be involved as a partner in a marriage *and* business. What should she do for the benefit of her family? Would we profit or lose if we sold the pedestal house? The question was unanswerable. She admitted the probability was that the pedestal house would lose money.

Karon had no knowledge of building costs or the house's salability. She liked the pedestal house and could appreciate it from an architectural standpoint, but if she were to live there, she didn't like the out-of-the-way location. Friends and conveniences were too distant. It meant interminable driving taking our three girls everywhere. She was an artist. Time was too precious to spend in the car. And so, to my ultimate sorrow as well as my sense of architectural accomplishment, my persuasiveness, *the-facts-of-the-matter* won the day. For financial security only, Karon decided she'd accept the sale of her beloved Amalfi house and move to the pedestal house.

SELLING THE AMALFI HOUSE

We put the house on the market with a 90-day escrow. The house was well located near stores and State Beach. We assumed prospective buyers would want to live there and waited a month or so, but no buyers came. Our pedestal house was nearly finished. At last, one month before we were to move in, we got a buyer. Somebody up there was looking out for us. Compared to what the Amalfi house had initially cost, prices had inflated and we made a substantial profit. Now all that remained before moving in was for our new pedestal house to be finished.

After his operation, Gordon had stayed about six months in Malibu and when things got more difficult had moved to Santa Monica. In the worst stages of his disease, headaches, sedatives, interminable sleeping, he was cared for by his personal miracle person, whoever she was, and I didn't see or hear from him after he moved to Santa Monica. Though cast down over this tragic turn of events, I was inundated with a business to run, the pedestal house to finish, three kids to raise, and a reluctant wife doing her best.

17. Doug, applying polyurethane to the columns.

A Tale of Two Houses

BUILDING DEPARTMENT

The pedestal house attracted the attention of the County Building Department personnel who occupied a portion of the new Malibu Civic Center directly below our house. Day-by-day the District Director and members of the Health Department, Planning Commission, County Road Department, Drainage Division, clerks and plan checkers, had a stunning view of the construction process of the house. The twelve, black, tapered steel beams cantilevering twelve feet in four directions from a wooden pedestal and supporting an underside of stucco and wood decking, excited curiosity. Every time I was at the counter, comments would be made about the growing construction. *How's the house coming? I see you've begun roof framing. Did the rains hurt the job?* I enjoyed building the new house and wanted to share the house more intimately with those who seemed interested. I decided to invite Department members over for lunch, perhaps Friday at noon. After checking with the District Director, I printed an announcement on letter-sized paper and put it on the wall near the Building Department counter. Friday morning I made coffee, set out cream and sugar, cups, saucers, stirring spoons, and was delighted when eight to ten especially invited Building Department members showed up for lunch. Young men and women, trudged up the hill in pairs or one by one, said their greetings, took a brief house tour, and finally settled on temporary chairs, or flopped on the deck to eat and enjoy the panoramic view. They complemented our work, amiably chatted, ate their brown-bag lunches, and had a relaxed break. Inviting them was an indication of my desire to be friendly and cooperative with those whom I wanted to please.

PEPSI COMMERCIAL

During construction, the Malibu pedestal house was attracting attention. Though I may be biased, I presumed everyone in his or her cars driving along the Coast Highway looked up in the hills and said, *"What's that?"* The unusual perfectly square house with a white double-pitched roof, topped at night by a glowing white skylight appeared as a round, illuminated disc ringed with warm glass that may have settled gently upon the Malibu hill from outer space. Cantilevered from its central column of clear-heart Redwood, the house looked, indeed, like *the Martians had landed!* It had a *flying saucer* appearance and some asked, *"Is that a toadstool house?"* I preferred the word *mushroom* house. At any rate, for those who took the time to look, a strange house in 1966, fully exposed and low on the hill in the heart of Malibu, was unusual to see. It excited comments, one way or the other, and was thought then to be, or at least I wanted it to be, representative of the wild, freethinking houses people of future Malibu would build.

While the house was yet uncompleted, cabinets built, but unpainted, finished parquet floor uninstalled, door hardware waiting, I was visited by two people entering our motor court in a black, top-down, Porsche. With sunglasses and breeze-ruffled hair, they got out of the car and introduced themselves. Removing his dark glasses, one of them said his company wanted to rent the house for two days at $400.00 to film a Pepsi-Cola commercial. They'd agree to leave the house spotlessly clean including, if necessary, sanding and retouching. Damages were guaranteed corrected to the owner's satisfaction.

Karon and I retired to talk privately. In a few minutes we decided to stop construction and take advantage of this adventurous idea. We both had to admit having our house on television would be good architectural publicity. I was not-too-secretly flattered it had been chosen. Also, we'd pick up the much-needed $400.00.

A couple of weeks later, television crews arrived with lighting equipment, cameras, sound men, actors, grips, a director, assistants, and tons of wires, frames and reflectors. At lunchtime from the street above, appetizing aromas drifted around and through three immense trucks and an assortment of cars. The first truck held equipment, the second, dressing rooms, the third, hot food and a catering crew. A generator rumbled quietly and switched on and off during the filming. Breakfast, lunch and dinner were served from an outdoors kitchen and serving stand beneath a wide umbrella. Casually dressed people milled in the street attending to affairs, some sitting on folding chairs eating and chatting under covered folding tables. Karon and I were astounded at so large and well-equipped an entourage.

An interested film historian and architect was a guest of the television group. His name was Bill Gleason, a handsome young man in his mid-thirties and well over six feet tall. He had a wonderfully deep voice and boyish brown hair that fell over one eye. He wore dark slacks, string-tied loafers, and an open-at-the-neck shirt. With hands in pockets, his manner was casual and his conversations lively. He often punctuated conversations with a deep laugh. Educated in architecture, but having been raised on the East coast as the only child of a distinguished father in radio, he had acquired a strong interest in the communication arts, radio, motion pictures, theater, and television. He also had a keen interest in educating others. Bill was quickly to become our close friend and because of mutual theatrical interests, he and Karon hit it off immediately. I felt honored and respected hearing complementary comments from an architecturally trained colleague about my pedestal creation.

18. Bill Gleason – architect, linguist, musician, movie historian.

As workmen went about setting up and selecting locations for the Pepsi commercial, the three of us stayed clear and observed. Making sure they were out of camera range, long, black wires were taped to the floor for sound and lighting equipment.

Wires were connected to a series of bright lights, recording and monitoring equipment and dangling microphones. Late in the afternoon Bill went up the hill and returned with a gallon of *Gallo* red wine. We smiled and watched while talking and joking and toasted each other in paper cups. After having had a toast or two too many, we grinned at each other and admitted the $2.50 gallon of wine was pretty good.

THEME

The theme of the commercial was:

(A young architect is completing his house and showing it off to his fiancée, or wife, or girl friend. As they make their rounds, the brilliance and profundity of the architect's design becomes overwhelming. They laugh and joke until that appropriate moment, (the point of the film), when they smile, gaze into each other's eyes, take up a can for a toast. "To the most wonderful elixir in the world, Pepsi-Cola."

The unspoken issue: *Brilliance of the architect. Implication: Only brilliant architects drink Pepsi-Cola. If you want to be a brilliant architect with a smashing girlfriend, drink Pepsi-Cola!*

I thought the part of the male lead was not yet cast. The director seemed to be looking over the heads of everyone for someone to play the architect. I extended myself to my full height, five-feet-seven-inches, casually crossed my legs, folded my arms, and leaned significantly against a doorjamb with a straight face. Within his full view I assumed the pose of what I thought was the gifted architect look. The director caught my eye, looked me up and down, and then quickly lost himself among the workmen. He came back with a boyish-looking young man about five foot ten, athletic, and dressed in clean Saturday clothes. His skin was golden brown from the sun and with a shock of hair carelessly over one eye; he wore an open-neck sports shirt with brown slacks and boots. As comedian Shelley Berman, says, *"He had a crooked smile, but straight teeth."* As it turns out the actor actually *was* a licensed architect from Long Beach and had been selected to play the lead alongside a cute, smiling, prom-queen type young lady. They performed successfully, I guess, but what did I know? As the song goes, *I tried, but I couldn't do it. I tried, but I couldn't do it. I tried…* I think I saw the commercial later, or may have heard from friends it had aired back east. We did get our $400.00 and they did leave the house clean.

HOUSE MOVE

There are a number of times in my life when I thought I'd pulled myself up by my bootstraps. *(Making something from nothing, then with courage, fortitude, hard work and hope, I'd continued to forge ahead.)* Every bit of money Karon and I made had been by hard work. How did I get into the new house? Either I was a hero seeing a window of opportunity and acting quickly, or I was a victim of fate and had acted without choice! What's the old line about *seeing the world as a cup that's half-full or a cup that's half-empty?* Perhaps

I was a hero *and* victim of fate. Characteristically, I see my cup as half-full.

We packed personal things of little monetary value into our two-year-old Volvo station wagon and made innumerable trips to and from the Amalfi Drive house to the Malibu house. Of course, for the whole family, moving into a new house *was* thrilling!

(The pedestal house stood strong, fresh, and clean, a stalwart beacon, braving itself against the sun, fog, and Santana winds. Sometimes billowy rain-clouds marched across a darkened ocean casting dazzling white patches across its dark, windblown face. The house stood there, forthright, head high; fearlessly protecting it's progenitors - the sensitive, honorable family within! Am I dreaming? Am I too exuberant?)

19. House during move-in period.

A Tale of Two Houses

After we left and new owners moved into our Amalfi house, the deed was done! That time was a benchmark, a milestone, and established an irrevocable commitment for our family to the new house. Moving into our spectacular new environment was exciting and distracted us from our sorrow over the loss of the Amalfi house. I, at least, dropped from my mind the idea of living in Santa Monica Canyon.

Shed like an old skin, the Amalfi house, also built for speculation, was easily behind me. My office had been in Malibu since January of 1958. It was now September of 1966. I'd been in Malibu eight years. For me, with office and home here too, life would be easier, and from a business standpoint, cheaper. Karon also was caught up in her new stay-at-home duties concerning children, finishing the house and becoming a Malibu wife. Viveka was taken out of her beloved Santa Monica Elementary School and put in first grade at Webster.

There was still the painting and finishing to do. On Saturdays and Sundays and after work I painted the interior walls while Karon finished the kitchen cabinets. I coated the beams, fascia, handrail and posts with two coats of Olympic 713 Brown Stain. The exterior redwood had two coats of clear Creosote. We ordered the most inexpensive floor we could buy, Oak Parquet in alternating six-inch squares. It took several months before everything would be completed. I made a hanging wood light fixture for the dining room table out of a 100-watt bulb and an upside-down Teak waste paper basket.

INTERIOR ARRANGEMENTS

Karon and I took the master bedroom and bath and installed our custom bed made for our Amalfi house by our good friend, Harry Heckendorf. It sat on casters for easy rolling and was constructed from 3/4" Douglas Fir plywood and wide Vertical Grain Douglas Fir stair treads. We brought and installed modest dressers and hung our clothes in the closet behind clear red birch sliding wardrobe doors. Viveka, Lilianne, and Amanda occupied a narrow single room designed so that later it could become two rooms. For the time being, Viveka *(6)* and Amanda *(2)* were to sleep in a double-decker bunk bed at one end of the room and Lilianne *(4)* in a low single bed at the other end. We installed and placed the brightly colored, but inexpensively made, children's furniture in their rooms. We brought our dining room table and chairs from the other house and meager living room furniture. All in all, though the house was joyful, the appointments were pathetic.

SPACE SHIP

20. The Starship has landed

At twilight one evening I made my way below the house. It was a calm evening with tall mustard weeds lining the narrow pathway to the geranium gardens. At an appropriate distance from the house, the ocean quiet and fading into the sky in growing darkness, I looked up and saw my design from an objective standpoint. Lighted from the inside, the *flying saucer house* rested quietly on the hillside and glowed like a magic starship. As the sun moved closer to the western horizon, the strange looking *ship* glowed with increasing intensity. It wasn't bright, but made its presence on the sloping hillside gently and forcefully known. The house was there. It claimed its space. There was no doubt. The *star ship* had landed.

WHILE SURFING

In the spring of 1967 I was surfing in home territory, which was of course, Surfrider Beach. Out on the point after work and waiting for waves, I sometimes chatted between breaks with fellow surfers. They asked if I lived in Malibu.

I said, "Yes."
"Where do you live?"
I'd point up to the house and say, *"Right there."*
They'd say, *"Where?"*
"There!" And I'd draw closer and align out my arm and finger for them.
"Wow!" They'd say. I expected they assumed if I lived in that gorgeous house I must be rich. I was embarrassed about owning so beautiful a house and being thought of as rich. I wasn't rich and I didn't feel rich. Perhaps I *was* rich, but not in money.

21. View to Surfrider Beach.

CHRISTMAS

Christmas struck us like the usual thunderbolt with our own family, Karon's parents *(Duke and Lois Conan)*, and Karon's brother, Dick. We muddled through. I made Christmas cards. We probably produced another *creatively* designed Christmas tree. *(We thought of ourselves as being modern, contemporary, and avant-garde. Though I have changed my beliefs over the years with a greater degree of appreciation for tradition, until that time we had never produced a standard Christmas tree.)* I did, however, string colored lights on the railings circling our floating house. While driving along Pacific Coast Highway in the early evening, I'd enjoy the sight of our beautiful house sparkling with Christmas lights on the hill and know that *that* was where my family was and that I'd soon be warm and at home.

LIVING

On the lower floor next to the circular stairway I arranged my conference table with my chair facing north to look past the motor court to the natural hillside beyond. I had three Herman Miller chairs, two orange non-roll types for clients, and a black one opposite for me with a tilt-rock, swivel action. I coined the catch phrase, *Tilt, Rock, Swivel and Roll with Doug Rucker.* I placed a layout table behind me and was, should good luck require, convertible to a drafting table. Then another drafting table for personal use overlooking Malibu Creek, mountains, Serra Retreat Monastery, geranium gardens, estuary, Surfrider Beach, Catalina, Palos Verdes and Movie Colony.

    A constant comment was, *"With a view like this, how do you get any work done?"* My reply was, *"Every time I look up, I get an instant vacation."*

    On the other side of the circular stairway were a file cabinet, bookshelves, and another layout-drafting table. With outstanding views, the design allowed a working space about half the size of a two-car garage. It was minimal, but if necessary would accommodate a principal and two draftsmen.

    Starting with a new office and landmark house, I wanted it to look the best and be the best. Early in 1967 I took it upon myself to purchase three expensive Herman Miller drafting stools. *($175.00 each)* They were built with a cast aluminum frame, wide foot ring, black Naugahide seats, and flexible back. The stools made a rich, solid sound as they clicked and clinked across the tile floor. It was a delight to come down to work in rank luxury, as it would be for my draftsmen if I were to have any.

    Unfortunately, Karon thought my stools purchase exorbitant and wished I'd spoken to her before buying them. Because of our increased financial burdens she thought I could have done just as well with more modest stools. She thought perhaps my enthusiasms were greater than my financial abilities. I thought buying the stools was a correct choice made from the gut. Though I must admit that when I wrote the order my forehead perspired and my armpits dampened. I reasoned, if I respect myself and respect my work then I must respect the *way* I work including my environment. I felt better about my newer self as a serious architect in practice in a serious house working on solidly constructed, well-designed stools rather than those of a more modest type.

22. Motor court showing two 1962 Volvos.

The stools would wordlessly tell prospective clients of my design ability; therefore I'd be more in demand. The unique house and quality stools would be lifetime assets. Our disagreement seemed an extension of other disagreements. Though Karon said she liked the house, it was still far from schools, close friends, theater, art shows, parents, musical activities, and stores. She was still objecting to spending far too much time in the car driving kids. A highly active person, Karon had places to go and things to do. Driving wasted her valuable life. In addition, now I was wasting money. I understood her point of view, but felt the new stools were necessary to my career as a modern architect. My choice proved correct over time and I was rewarded on a day-to-day basis by their utility, comfort and durability.

PERSONAL RESOURCES DRAINED

I was making a comfortable living when Gordon and I began the house for speculation in 1964. During 1965 and Gordon's illness and while finishing the house my practice was doing decidedly worse. In the latter part of 1966 when we moved into the new house, my income was impossibly low. From the end of 1964 to the end of 1966 my gross slipped from $19,000.00 a year to less than $7,500.00 and yearly mortgage payments to Glendale Federal were $4,092.00. My *net* income was $2,423.00, *severely less* than our mortgage payments. There was nothing remaining for food, water, gas, electricity, health insurance, pediatrics, dental, lunch-money, food, clothes, laundry, car payments, car and house gas and insurance, emergencies and certainly no savings for our second trust deed payment.

If Gordon and I had finished our house for speculation with the market in the doldrums, we would have been making *no* profit. Since we depended on impossible building projects in Malibu, we'd have earned *no* income. Fate would have forced us to rent our spectacular house at a pittance to cover part or all of the two mortgages.

I am eternally sorry fate dealt Gordon a mortal blow, but a lesser fate decreed Karon and I take over the partnership's job. That meant Karon and our three children were dependent on an architect who depended on client's building, who depended on lenders, of which there weren't any of either. In 1966 I netted $2,423.00. This was not enough to support a family of five in a new house in the heart of Malibu. Fate handed the Rucker family a severe financial difficulty.

23. Rich house of the poor. (Picture from the Mallen lot.)

HOW WE LIVED

I have been asked, *"Doug, how did you get through 1966 – 1967?"* With many warnings during those years from Glendale Federal we sometimes missed as many as three mortgage payments. We were lucky that Glendale and most lending institutions were reluctant to add yet another house to their already packed foreclosure list. Lenders during a buyers market developed a policy of leniency toward indebted owners. It would cost the banks and lending institutions too much money to foreclose and sell below cost.

We allowed our property taxes to lapse for an extended period. *(Perhaps as much as four years.)* On the back sheets of the Malibu Times we were embarrassed and disheartened to read our address under the *Delinquent Property Taxes List*. At that time the State would allow us to remain seven years on the delinquent list before taking action. The State couldn't afford to foreclose on our property and other than interest, our second trust deed was not due until the middle of 1968. Also, in finishing the house during 1967, we were six to eight months late in paying three sub-contractors. Eventually we did pay them and remained friends. Our tax deductions were high since most of our mortgage was interest. Still, life wasn't easy.

LIVING IN THE HOUSE

I have tried to remember what living in the house was like in the financially slim times of 1966 and 1967. I was worried. Since our extreme financial problem was continually evident, the things I remember are things my organism wants to forget because those were hard times. Our family had nothing. Being poor, of course, is relative; we were suffering in *Malibu*. To all appearances we lived in an expensive, dramatic house. Our family looked rich. Our children were three, five and seven. Viveka was enrolled with youngsters from relatively affluent families at Webster Elementary. Years later talking about schooling, our children told us they didn't know why they had so little compared to friends who had so much, particularly since they seemed to live in a better house. I don't know about their school experiences, but I assume having to wear hand-me-downs, well-washed clothes, worn shoes and being unable to buy lunch embarrassed them. *(They always brought their own lunch and bought fresh milk to drink.)* One daughter complained she was sometimes humbled to ask a friend if she could share her lunch, though I can't for the life of me imagine myself sending my child off to school without lunch and milk money.

In 1967 Karon joined the PTA. Lili and Amanda attended pre-school operated by Verne Riggle at the Malibu Presbyterian Church. Verne was the wife of the local Health Inspector, Dave Riggle. We had acquired a delightful, much loved, medium-sized *"international"* dog named Daisy. She was sweet and loving and was eventually surprised and delighted with her own doggy door. We also acquired a couple of Siamese cats, Suki and Ratface.

At night we'd hear the shrill yelps of young coyotes

battling for a portion of the evenings kill. Sometimes in the early morning or after midnight we'd hear the relentless crashing, hiss, pause, and breaking of waves on the shores of Surfrider Beach and the Movie Colony. On sunny summer Sundays, the steady, white-noise roar of cars on Pacific Coast Highway was in the background and an ambulance siren screaming two or three times a day was common.

There was the proverbial rattlesnake that slithered up on our motor court and coiled itself outside our sliding glass door. I don't like to kill rattlesnakes, but did so because of the danger to the children and Daisy. Such were a portion of our living experiences in the early years of family life in the pedestal house.

24. Finished Upper Deck.

A Tale of Two Houses

THE PEDESTAL HOUSE

After a sound sleep and waking in the wee hours of the morning, the full moon quietly and brilliantly lighted our house, the hills, the broad fields of geraniums and Malibu Creek Estuary. I was astounded at days end by the variety of cloud miracles that spread themselves across the sky. When the moon was rising and the sun not yet set, we'd see two of earth's vital orbs timelessly suspended, mysterious and immovable at opposite reaches of the sky. On days with offshore winds and a setting sun, the ocean water was colored in smooth, darkening shades of blue and purple. On usual days the westerly wind in the early afternoon blew until 6:00 p.m. then died and left us with a comfortable evening. During the rainy season, the heavy clouds advancing quickly down the coast brought with them, as if directed by God, shafts of sunlight playing in spherical patches of light and luminous contrasts across the ocean's surface.

The pedestal house, conscious of every nuance and subtlety of wind, was like a kite strung in the air. It knew every atmospheric condition and resisted the wind's power and lashings of rain. Sometimes on a quiet evening a moist breeze carrying the warm, rank smell of damp leaves would sweep indifferently past the house on its way to the sea. At those times I'd be transported to a northern Indiana lake in mid-summer, or an arrival at the Honolulu airport where the air is charged with negative ions and coming rain. This movement of dampish air introduced off-shore Santa Ana winds that eventually blew in gusts of 60 or 70 miles-an-hour. They scoured Malibu Canyon of it's moisture and blew unapologetically through and around our house. When the force of the winds struck, the house would howl and whine like a restless dog. A slightly cracked sliding door produced a variety of shrieks and whistling sounds that not only rattled the brain but rattled the soul. In Santa Ana air Karon and I became restless and apprehensive. Its dryness and positive ions kept us awake. There was no sleeping in the pedestal house during these heavy winds; only lying awake thinking, watching, turning over, listening.

At night when heavy winds pounded against the black windows with gusts of fifty or sixty miles an hour the fixed glass panels would flex and bow. More than once I watched and expected the windows to blow out and let cold winds violate our room. Sometimes during a particularly windy night I'd sit motionless in the dining room, elbows on the table, chin in hands and stare at our hanging Teak lamp. I knew the ceiling was over forty-feet above the ground and that any movement of the house would reflect itself in the movement of the ceiling and therefore in the hanging lamp. Like a pendulum, if the lamp began to swing even imperceptibly, it would be caused by the movement of the house. I didn't want a moving lamp or a moving house. I focused on the hanging lamp during the heaviest of the winds and never saw the lamp so much as twitch. I was convinced, the house, for all it's high-strung, kite-like quality, resisted the winds like a rock

On a promontory with the land sloping away in three directions, the house was blatantly exposed to the elements. From all directions the pedestal house was subject to sun, wind, fog, rain and fire. The vulnerability of the house exacerbated my own vulnerability. Sometimes my imagination would take hold and I'd visualize strong Santa Ana winds blowing our whole house off the hill with me watching while it tumbled down, skylight over footings, to land upside down in the geraniums with caissons in the air.

During hard rain the windows were pelted not only vertically or diagonally, but horizontally, or even worse, raindrops slung along by strong winds would drive up our hill and attack us from below. Rain would drive *up* at us. How weird was that? Such days were dim and gloomy and leaks would appear in the southwest corner. Sometimes the house seemed to ride on the mist. I'd sit around the fireplace in a drizzling cloud and realize moisture wasn't falling on me. I was warm and dry while the pedestal house sat secure and contentedly as part of the mist.

But when the air was still and it was Sunday morning I'd don a baseball cap, pull up a deck chair and sit outside with a peanut butter sandwich and cold milk. I'd relax with my feet up and eat and bask and marvel at fifty or sixty sailboats cutting through the water beyond the pier, leaning on the wind, dipping and slanting in the afternoon breeze.

Sailboats would plunge and rise and drive into the westerlies then laboriously round the buoy, sails full and white, the ships tentative with sails flopping while coming about and beginning a swift reach for the marina and home. On any warm Sunday the house was a tower in heaven looking down on the world; the ultimate in happiness, relaxing and basking in the sun.

MONEY

One evening I quickly fell asleep, but awakened well after midnight in a state of anxiety. Again I was thinking I had no money. Our mortgage payment was two months behind. Our refrigerator held little food. High in our master bedroom I threw off blankets, sat up and looked out the window over our short deck to the mountain on the other side of Malibu Creek. It was pitch-black and its ridge cut sharply across the overcast sky. Beyond the range of black mountains and along Pacific Coast Highway a thin string of lights flickered silently and winked as they diminished all the way to Santa Monica and beyond. In the farther distance five or six smokestacks from the Hyperion plant rose above the broader plane of Redondo Beach. Huge volumes of steam billowed from their spouts and moved soundlessly and aimlessly in the air before evaporating. A miniature light from a 747, like a distant bee, blinked and moved steadily to a late night landing at LAX. Karon was asleep. The children's room was still. The dog and cats were curled in their favorite places on the foot of the kid's beds. The night was black and muggy. I knew of no place to borrow money nor any place to turn. I lay back in my bed, the back of my hand on my forehead and stared at the ceiling.

After a while I dozed off and my mind drifted to a place in childhood. I was eight years old in our tiny Lombard house in Illinois. I remembered how safe I felt. Little brother Dave and I were in our miniscule bedroom in our isolated house in the middle of the Lombard fields. We had two mulberry trees in front, a detached garage off to the side, a deep backyard with a well, and to the rear, a lone elm. In my thoughts it was also after midnight and I was sleeping with my head on a pillow propped against the sill of a partly opened window. My mother and father loved me. I loved them. It comforted me to smell the soft night breezes through the slightly opened window. I listened for a while and in the distance heard the rumbling of thunder. A common storm was rinsing its way across the midwest. It would soon pass over our home. I remember a lull, then a breeze and a quickly brightened window, darkness momentarily, then the rumble of thunder. Soon thick droplets struck our light roof, then a rush of rain, a pause, then more rain. All through the night an accelerating roar rattled and danced on the roof. It gradually increased, softened, then came with a violence and sometimes died to a whisper. It was steady, but the storm was not as powerful as others. I was warm and dry and peaceably lulled to sleep and woke now and then to experience the spattering of tiny raindrops on my face and remember I was warm under the covers and loved where I was.

As this dreamy reminiscence ended, I was awakened by *California raindrops* lightly striking our roof. Water from the sky rolled off our roof, dripped from the eaves, splashed on the rounded railings and blackened our deck boards. A cooler breeze filled our room and soon rain whipped and pounded and caressed our sky-high house. We were warm and dry like I was as a child. I sighed and my eyelids closed. Rain was the gift from God when I needed it the most. I thanked the eternal forces for this welcome relief, forgot my troubles, and slept like a contented eight-year-old for the remainder of the night.

KARON

The most difficult period of Karon's adjustment was from late 1966 to late 1968 while she tried to attune herself to Malibu life. It was hard for Karon to depend on a man who didn't seem to have a steady income, particularly because she had three small children in an isolated location, was not a breadwinner and felt helpless. Being an accomplished person in acting, singing, sculpting, weaving, and swimming with an academic intelligence, she was also ambitious. She felt trapped. She did not want to devote her time exclusively to family needs. Karon had the brains, talent, and motivation to pursue her interests and was unhappy if she could make no progress toward them.

25. Karon smiling.

(Karon was rapidly becoming a serious fiber artist making large and small colorful and artistic weavings. I designed and made a ten-foot high by eight-foot wide loom from one-inch dowels on a vertical grain Douglas Fir frame. I'm not sure if it was ever used.)

In early 1967 when we were so desperately in need of money, Karon recurrently dreamed military planes were bombing and strafing our house. Her family was in mortal danger and she would awaken disturbed and depressed. According to the children at odd times they would come upon their mother weeping. She didn't confide in them and though she sometimes spoke to me of her dreams, I never saw her weep and I don't remember her in as much despair. I knew some of what was wrong. My income was low and our future unresolved. Karon was a stay-at-home mom, frustrated at not finding the time to pursue her passionate calling of singing and fiber-art.

While living in what some would call a *dream house,* the old quote goes, *"If Momma ain't happy, ain't nobody happy."* Momma was unhappy. The Rucker family struggled hard adjusting to a relative state of poverty.

We *did* pursue one thing Karon loved to do. We kept singing. We still belonged to the Neo Renaissance Singers headquartered in Pacific Palisades and when our rehearsals were there we hired a baby sitter and were gone for the evening. When rehearsals were at home we needed no baby sitter and our small group of six or eight sang downstairs next to the circular stairway around Lili's small upright piano.

As time went on Karon involved herself in Webster Elementary as an after-school teacher. She taught Arts and Crafts to grades first through fifth. Bringing Mandy, she could be at school when Viveka and Lilianne were let out of classes and able to supervise them while teaching. She helped after school students make plaster casts, paint plastic plates, mold statues, do weavings with colored string and driftwood and paint watercolors using hands for brushes. She also helped her youngsters make Christmas and Valentine cards and Halloween decorations.

Knowing after school students, she became acquainted with their mothers and fathers and while the parents picked up their children she enjoyed talking with them and encouraging them about their children. Being familiarized with younger students led to giving private swimming lessons to preschoolers in the Serra Retreat area and Malibu Park. Many youngsters benefited from Karon's efforts in both her after-school programs and swimming instruction. Despite Malibu's seeming inconveniences, Karon was getting acquainted and adapting herself to her Malibu life away from Santa Monica Canyon.

FUNERAL

Sometime in 1968 Gordon Ewert died. Held in a Santa Monica church, I went to the funeral with Tony De Vivo. Gordon's former wife, son, and mother were there, of course, but I don't remember meeting them. If I did, it was only briefly. Perhaps, I saw them in the first row when the pastor was giving his talk, but I don't remember having seen or talked to them. In fact I remember little of what the pastor said. It seemed a typically religious ceremony. There was mention of Gordon's passing on *to a far better place* and that he'd led a loving, productive life and would be severely missed by his family and friends. The pastor's rather extensive talk was interspersed with many short verses read from the bible and commingled with religious music. As much as I appreciated the pastor's effort, for me the talk didn't reflect the Ewert I knew. There was little mention of his prowess in skiing, photography, construction, lobster diving, bonsai hobby, gliding, sense of humor, philosophy, ownership of an apartment built by himself, or his great enthusiasm for people and life.

Perhaps my memory is not perfect, but I don't remember mention of his war efforts. Certainly his World War II experiences, such as putting his life on the line for America, were an important part of his life; one he never forgot and one that forced him to use every bit of human skill of which he was so plentifully endowed. Despite the inhumanity of man in all wars, there was also heroism in the war. I would have to count Gordon a true hero. Perhaps I'm a victim of selective listening, but other things the pastor said did not catch my ear. What the pastor did say might have been important to his mother, son, and former wife. If so, I do not begrudge the pastor his sermon or the feelings of his immediate family.

DICK HAINES

While we lived in our Santa Monica Canyon house, oil-painter Dick Haines and his wife lived in a contemporary house downhill and directly across the street. He was also the head of the painting department at the Otis Institute of Design and a significant and popular Southern California artist who made a career teaching and selling paintings. He was often published in national Art magazines, including John Entenza's Southern California *Arts and Architecture* magazine. For our new Malibu pedestal house we bought his *Peasant Girl*.

In celebration of our new house Dick gave us a cartoon; a working drawing for one panel of the thirteen tile mosaic panels surrounding the upper floor of the four-story UCLA music building. The mural depicted the history of music and this single panel was called *The Gospel Singers*. In working on the project Dick would do smaller scale paintings of the entire mural then transpose them to full-size for a tile contractor who, on scaffolds, would then embed them four stories high on exterior walls. Architect, artist, and craftsman worked together for a unified building. Each artist was vital to the other in bringing about a true marriage of art and architecture.

Though indeed he never suspected as much, I received an artistic education from Dick. Knowing him allowed me to feel what it was like to be in the art field. He was an inspiration to me and showed me a similar path for myself.

26. Peasant Girl. (Size - 30in x 40in)

POSSIBLE TEACHING PROFESSION

While work was low and worry was high the idea of going to work for another architect was unappealing to me. I didn't want to play second to anyone, not even a respected architect. Karon knew this and became intensely worried which was understandable because her family was in crisis and I was the only means to a viable solution – money. She suggested strongly and repeatedly I give serious consideration to teaching at UCLA or Southern

27. Cousin Kathy Rucker with a five-foot by eight-foot cartoon/mural of The Gospel Singers by neighbor and friend Dick Haines. This cartoon is one of thirteen panels surrounding the UCLA Music Building depicting the history of music.

California University. Predisposed to academics, she was a good student in art, music, theater arts, and intellectual pursuits. A graduate of the upper class Pomona College, having her master's degree in Theater Arts and Art from UCLA and having been for two years the personal secretary for Dr. Freud, head of the UCLA Theater Arts department, she was comfortable in the University setting. Though I wasn't comfortable in that setting, I could see her taking pride as the talented, educated wife of a University architectural professor.

Not that my innate talents would allow me to teach. I questioned how I could be a professor with only a Bachelor of Science from a four-year out-of-state school, even if the school was a good one. Teaching was anathema to me.

I could not imagine myself at forty years old in front of a class attempting to teach twenty year olds with their varying intelligence, attitudes and enthusiasms. I feared they might know more than me and stump me with impossible questions. I wouldn't know what to do in front of a class. I'd have to make lesson plans. How does one do that? I'd have to teach what I already knew. How interesting is that? I'd feel the inadequate fool! I was still unsure of my *own* work. I considered I had only a *developing* architectural philosophy and had not yet come to terms with how capable I was or how I'd proceed in business for myself. Though I felt adequate with people on a one to one basis, I was mortally afraid of being the center of attention; terrified of leading and speaking in front of a group. With no teaching degree and years of study to get one, I imagined I'd be summarily rejected. Was it not true that *"Those who do, do! Those who can't, teach!"* I tried to stay viable in the community through infrequent contacts with real estate agents, local organizations and the Building Department. My unalterable self-image was that of a *boy-architect going it alone*. My soul rejected the profession of teaching!

Instead, I went surfing. I surfed Surfrider Beach and the Latigo break. I remember driving home in my black Volvo with a waxed, dripping board on the rack, shivering, with droplets of salt water drying on my face, bare feet scattering sand on the floor mats and feeling peaceful and exercised. Exercise reduced emotional anxiety. It was easier not to teach. While I wasn't working I did other things around the house.

On Saturdays I'd don my Levis and loose T-shirt and depart to the steep slope below to work on fire protection trimming native brush and sumac. I'd sit beneath the ten-foot sumac bush and trim high enough to walk below. In gloves and clippers on the easterly slope with brown work shoes digging in against the rocks and dirt, I'd trim the huskier branches, ripping off slim ones by hand. I'd saw thicker trunks and throw them aside in a pile for later pick-up. I disliked removing brush because the branches had to be clipped small enough to fit into plastic trash-bags and dragged up the hill.

Some days with a pick and shovel I moved laterally along the hillside down by the telephone pole to make pathways or *bunny-trails* to negotiate below on the steeply sloping half-acre. Watching carefully for poison oak and rattlesnakes I worked the trails to a rocky edge that sloped more steeply into a ravine. At times, out of sight under an overhanging sumac, I'd sit down to rest, gather my wind and dream about a future time when I might build a guest house spanning our thirty-foot barranca.

28. A Christmas card filled with fury, passion and anxiety, 1967

Mentally I'd work out a simple glass-enclosed living space on a bridge across the barranca. It would have a double-pitched roof and maybe a skylight with a wide redwood deck cantilevered dramatically into space. It'd have a bath in the back, space for an in-line kitchen, dining counter, and maybe a small, sculpturally formed, contemporary metal fireplace.

(Fire-Drum) I'd create harmony. Lost in impractical dreams, I'd eventually return to the house for a peanut butter and banana sandwich on fresh white bread and a cold glass of milk with maybe a cookie for desert. I sweated! I worried! I worked! I enjoyed being outside, but life was difficult!

YARD WORK

During heavy early spring rains a portion of the hillside above our steep driveway had begun to move and slide leaving loose earth and weedy sod draining messily down our driveway. With pick and shovel I fashioned a narrow channel from the source and guided it toward a catch basin I made of concrete. By installing an underground four-inch pipe from the catch basin, I was able to direct the water swiftly to the driveway. Once in the driveway it flowed to a narrow, twelve-foot long strip-grating that crossed the pavement and intercepted driveway storm water before entering the motor court. From there it was conducted down-slope through an eight-inch diameter corrugated metal drainpipe to a rock outflow well below the house.

There were *free* trees to plant. In 1968 the fire department operated a nursery off Malibu Canyon Road near Piuma Drive where anyone could get up to ten one-gallon pine trees to plant for erosion control. *(I don't know how the fire department feels about their former generosity, since all pine trees are now considered a fire hazard. These days, sometimes the fire department requires owners to remove pine trees.)*

I picked up ten aleppo pines in ten-gallon cans and planted them dutifully around the property. Two were to flank our driveway near the strip grating next to the motor court. We watered them and they continued to grow for our remaining time there. Our lives were like the aleppo's: *in process and context.* Growing while everything else was happening.

TOOL SPACE

I had intended the open space beneath the house to be enclosed with safety glass for office space. But a forced air furnace sat fairly hidden under the house and blew heated air up through plastic ducts into floor registers above. A seventy-gallon water heater sat next to the furnace on a three-foot square concrete slab. A container case and suction tubes for our built-in vacuum cleaner hung from a wall supporting the motor court. Close up, the affect of the utility units shrouded in wires and ducts was not a pretty sight. But, seen from a distance, the unsightly units disappeared in the shadows and thankfully did not show up in photographs.

In the shadows beneath the house next to the utility units seemed a good place to make a small workshop. I built a little table along the backside of the easterly shear-wall with two shelves over. Between the table and shelves I installed hooks and nails to hang hammers, saws, drills, shears, clippers, wrenches, a hand-scythe, etc. On shelves I stored paint pans, brushes, rags, varnish, polyurethane and turpentine solvent. To the north under the motor court I hung picks, shovels, brooms, crowbars, weed-whackers and other brushing equipment. The under floor space was ideally located adjacent to sloping land that always needed working.

HOME LIFE

In 1967 our daughters were seven, five, and three. Viveka was attending second grade at Webster Elementary, Lilianne was in kindergarten, and Amanda was in Verle Riggle's Preschool Day Care Program at the Malibu Canyon Presbyterian Church. Amanda was doing cutting, pasting, watercolors, clay projects, taking naps, singing Itzy Bitzy Spider and pursuing numerous children's activities, including cut-outs, pasting, and listening to stories. Karon picked each of the children up at various times of the day and that made chaos of Karon's schedule. An active and energetic person, Karon just couldn't get into a creative project before she'd be interrupted. None of this was the children's fault. Thirty-five years later, with humorous conviction and a bit of irony, my stepson *Chris Lewi* would describe past dilemmas of this sort: *"That's the way how it was!"*

Karon was a night person and I've always been a day person. On weekdays I'd be the one to make sure the children's brown-bag lunches were made with a cartoon usually drawn on one side and see Viveka and Lili off to school. On Sunday's I'd sometimes be up with Vivi and Lili and we'd be very quiet in the morning so as not to wake Amanda or Karon and we'd watch cartoons for an hour on our black and white kitchen TV.

On weekends I'd sometimes take the children for a walk down one of our two overgrown rutted roads toward the beach leading to the geranium gardens. Sometimes I'd take Vivi and Lili to Whizzin's, a restaurant on Agoura Road between the Cheesebro and Kanan exits near the Ventura Freeway. Amanda was yet too small. We ordered pancakes, eggs, and bacon with orange juice or milk to drink. I remember my two attractive young daughters sitting neat and clean opposite me with their heads just above the counters. These infrequent episodes at Whizzin's with my two wonderful daughters were a special experience for a young father with financial worries in a depressed career-building stage. I wish I'd taken them more often, but life was tough and time and money insufficient.

Sometimes Karon and I would take the whole family to Surfrider Beach or to a little private cove off the Old Malibu Road we owned jointly with members of the Malibu Knolls Property Owner's Association. Earth from our little portion of the twenty-foot bluff was continually sliding on to a rocky beach. However in random areas there were patches of sand big enough to hold a beach blanket. It was there we settled. The surf-line didn't have a sandy bottom but was covered with dark rounded rocks and eelgrass. Nevertheless, we walked a hundred yards or so to sandier areas and bodysurfed over sand *and* rocks and had fun at *our* beach.

BEDTIME STORIES

When it was bedtime the children would ask me to tell them a story. This happened every night and though I was always tired from a full day I usually made up a story just so I could get on with the evening. The stories settled around themes derived from comic strip characters in Walt Kelly's *Pogo* and a song I'd known since high school called *The Monkey and the Buzzard*. A portion of the lyrics:

The buzzard took the monkey for a ride in the air.
The monkey thought that everything was on the square.
But the buzzard tried to throw the monkey off of his back.
And the monkey straightened up and said now, 'Listen Jack!
Straighten up and fly right!
Straighten up and fly right!
Straighten up and stay right!
Cool down Papa, don't ya blow your top!

In my bedtime stories the monkey *(protagonist)* would stroll down a pathway that meandered through a flood plain of wild flowers and weeds to the lake. Monkey would always pick up a friend like Bob the rabbit or Bitzy the squirrel. *(The monkey had to talk to someone.)* Midway to the lake there was an alligator dozing under the foliage with his tail across the path. He was agitated when the monkey and his friends continually tripped over his tail provoking a dialogue of humorous comments.

A Tale of Two Houses

"Wow! You did it again! Can't you watch where you're goin?"
 "Sorry Mr. Alligator, we was jus' talkin' an…"
"Look where you're goin' nex' time!"
 "OK, Mr. Alligator. Say! Could you give us a ride to the lake?".
'Ahm sleepin'!'
 "Well. You ain't now!"
Heaven's to Betsy! What does an alligator have to do to get some shut-eye?"
 "You been sleepin' for three days."
"Ahm hungry!"
 "Don't look at us."
Etc. Etc. Etc.

They always excused themselves and could never see the alligator's tail or remember it was there or were too preoccupied in their conversations to watch for it and so in each story continued to trip over it. The alligator though, after his initial outbursts, was quite a friendly guy. He was not *always* hungry like alligators are supposed to be and after numerous comic dialogues, complaints, and caustic replies, he often took his wild friends for a ride on his back to adventures in the lake.

At the lake they'd meet talking turtles and fish's or a friendly frog who'd hop high in the air, plunk in the water, and swim like lighting beneath the surface, or he'd dive deep down pushing with his long green legs into the black watery depths. Sometimes the alligator dog-paddling with long strokes of his arms and flat feet would swim deep into the pond and the monkey and his friends would meet usually friendly aquatic inhabitants down there, like turtles, clams, and sleepy catfish feeding lazily on the bottom. We didn't worry about breathing under water and though it would have been dark, we could always see well enough.

BABY SITTERS

On occasion Karon and I would go out to dinner or to the theater or to visit friends. Our preferred sitter was Karon's mother, Lois, but when she wasn't available we had other sitters. Our most frequent alternative was a seventeen-year-old neighbor called Lolly. The kids loved Lolly. The children and she could easily identify with each other. For the same reasons the girls also got along well with Lolly's nineteen-year-old sister, Suzy. When neither Lolly nor Susy was available the elderly Mrs. Gonzalez would stay. She worried us slightly because she had only peripheral vision. Her retina - the center of her eye - was damaged. She could not focus as we do. However she was diligent, loving, and like a grandmother to the kids. What more could parents ask? We called her often during our absence to make sure everything was OK. The children seemed to like Mrs. Gonzales and when we returned before midnight everything was in order.

DRINKING

Our friend Bill Gleason visited for dinner a few times a year. Sometimes we invited ten or fifteen other friends and Bill would set up a screen and projector with reels of film and we'd watch an old movie like *It Happened One Night* with Claudette Colbert and Clark Gable, or *Northwest Passage,* with Cary Grant, or the *Wizard of Oz,* with Judy Garland and her Oz friends. Bill always brought cheap wine and we drank it in good humor to celebrate good spirits.

I'd never tasted wine until I was thirty and hadn't formed any kind of drinking habit. But when the Pepsi commercial was videotaped and Bill had brought over his gallon of Gallo he'd bought for two dollars and fifty cents, I began to think, erroneously, that drinking wine like smoking cigarettes was a mature activity. Wouldn't it be better to be a man-architect than what I'd always thought of myself as a boy-architect?

I thought drinking wine would make me mature. If I smoked and drank and was married, certainly I was mature and could call myself a man. Drinking would make me feel grown up. When Bill was there I'd drink wine. Then one day I decided to buy wine for dinner. Karon and I would share a bottle of wine and soon wine became a regular thing. I'd have a glass of wine and sometimes Karon would have a glass. Then we'd both have another glass with dinner. After dinner, since the bottle was almost gone anyway, I'd finish it off and then fall asleep for an early evening nap. Mild intoxication relieved my financial situation and became what I thought to be a harmless habit

PHOTOS OF PEDESTAL HOUSE

After a year or so, business slowly returned and while I was working on the Anderson and Davis houses, Dan McMasters called with an invitation to publish the pedestal house in the *Home* section of the Los Angeles Times. I was delighted! Dan had arranged again for Dick Gross to photograph the house. After a number of calls, Dick and I decided to photograph the house on a weekday in the late fall of 1968.

    I asked, *"Dick, how do you know that particular day will be a good day for shooting?"*

    He said, *"Like all jobs, we'll take our chances."*

    When that fall day arrived I got up in the dark an hour before sunrise. Since I was to be Dick's assistant I dressed in Levi's, sweatshirt and brown leather work-boots. While the sky was still gray I ate a bowl of cold cereal. Dick arrived well before sunup. He wanted to catch the sun's first rays and went right to work below the house setting up his tripod. He had an eight-by-ten camera with a black hood and a lens that showed everything upside down. The big camera was for a foreshortened, dramatic shot looking upward toward the underside of the house. It revealed black steel beams splaying from the pedestal with white stucco between. He used endless amounts of time making test shots with his Polaroid camera, studying each with a professional's eye.

I learned colored photographs had to be especially lighted in case they were printed in black and white. He took so long taking and examining the Polaroid's we both became anxious we'd miss the arrival of the sun's first rays. It seemed any moment the sun would spring from the horizon and we'd not be ready. Dick hoped the light glancing off the gray ocean from behind the Palos Verdes Peninsula would bestow a quiet color to the surrounding terrain that would reflect powerfully on our subject. It was the last second. The set-up was perfect. The sun was ready to peek over the top. Dick held the shutter-button with connecting wire to the camera in one hand and glanced many times to the house, then to the camera, then toward breaking dawn. With cocked thumb and the precise moment he'd press the shutter-button.

In that magic time before he clicked I felt and saw an aura that surrounded the pedestal house. It included the camera and the two of us standing in reverent silence. Our subject and we were magically surrounded by a special glow. I was enthralled. I supposed Dick was enthralled. The house was enveloped in mystery. The aura was golden with meaning. His timing was perfect and in that special moment, like pressing the button for lift-off, he quietly clicked. The shot was over. Fold up the tripod. Collect the gear. Move to next shot. There seemed to be no time for a letdown experience, but I had one anyway.

We made several more exterior shots, Dick checking the Polaroid's, getting the light perfect, moving away from the camera, finger on shutter button, feeling the aura, and quietly taking the picture. In the early afternoon Dick moved inside, this time using a four-by-five camera and brilliant theatrical lights. Again, there was much maneuvering, meticulous adjustments including moving or removal of furniture or accessories, waiting for that magic moment and

A Tale of Two Houses

the silent anti-climax of pressing the shutter-button.

After finishing the inside, we moved down to the bottom of the hill for an outside photograph. This time the pedestal house was reflected in the setting sun against the mountains. I was in the bushes in the foreground and had my picture taken with the house in the background. I loved being an assistant for Dick and cared for him as a kind, artistic and dedicated person. I respected him and enjoyed watching him with his creative eye.

One time I asked if he would enjoy having a piece of artwork or sculpture; some *thing* of beauty to respond to on a daily basis. I did not offer him *my* artwork, but I wanted to know if ownership of artful things was important to him. I thought for one so involved with composition, colors and creativity, he'd certainly want to surround himself with beautiful objects. He said, *"No. I'm already aware of beauty. My thirst for beautiful things is continually quenched by my work. I see all the art and beauty I need through my lens."*

Sometime later before Dick moved to Ojai, he mailed me negatives of all the photos he'd done of my work. For the Home section of the L. A. Times, he'd photographed the Halliburton's, Moule's, Larsen's, Knebel's, Dutcher's, and his last work, the Rucker's. I was proud to be his personal assistant for each job. I learned from him. He gave me whatever photography education I have.

ADAMSON COMMISSION

After two years living in the pedestal house and having published several other houses, I was gaining special acknowledgement from the community. In public, at the market, or after the theater and being introduced to someone new, the conversation having turned to where we lived, people would say, *"Oh! You're the one who lives in the mushroom house!"* I would lower my eyes, hands in pockets, kick the dust, and modestly admit, *"Yeah! I'm the one."*

Numerous Malibu people knew me. I was beginning to have a *hey-day*. I'd done publishable work and lived in that special house, *"...the one that looks like a flying saucer."* Because I'd been working successfully and honestly in Malibu for ten years and having been a consultant for the Marblehead Land Company, the owners, Rhoda May, Sylvia Neville and Merritt Adamson had enough confidence in me to give me one of my most prized commissions. The Company was planning the Point Dume Mobile Home Park on a bluff overlooking the ocean to the south and to the west Zuma Beach.

The Adamson's wanted the building to reflect Malibu's Spanish heritage. That meant it had to have the massive white *Mission* look with tile roofs, tile floors and huge beams. They hoped to embed murals in the interior drywall and exterior stucco. The tile would be what they'd saved from the old Malibu Tile Company since historical days. I was somewhat disconcerted since my training and love for architecture centered on the more contemporary, mid-century, post-and-beam style. I loved the indoor-outdoor designs, the bare *(but beautiful)* bones approach and to build environments for living rather than a series of square voids to be furnished later. My motto was, *"What you see is what you get."* To do the job at all meant I'd have to work the two styles together, the Mission look and the post-and-beam look, an always difficult but I hoped not impossible task.

The program consisted of a 6,000 square foot Recreation Complex with covered parking for twenty-four cars, two duplexes around a fifty-foot pool and spa, pool changing and equipment room with bathrooms for men and women, a coin-operated Laundromat, plus entry Guard House and Gates and, unbelievably, in 1969 it was to cost a total of $185,000.00.

For a short period, I hired the Augustson brothers, Clyde full time and Clyde's brother at part time to work on the Doerner and Larson houses, while I devoted my time exclusively on the Adamson project.

Letter - January 6, 1969
Dear Mother and Dad,
Probably the reason I have not written much in this past year is because of the pressures of work. In 1968 I had the best year I've ever had from a business standpoint. So far 1969 looks like it may be as good. I did over a dozen jobs in '68. They are all working out well and as their jobs are finishing construction, each owner is still smiling.

The house (of ours) will be published in the L. A. Times Home section on the 9th of February. I will be getting the house on the cover in a very dramatic shot and will get six pages inside. It should be very good for me from a business standpoint and it is, I guess, some measure of appreciation for all the hours of work and anxiety. I think it was worth it.

Also in February the Knebel house in Calabasas (Monte Nido) will be coming out in the Better Homes and Garden's annual Idea Book. The Idea Book is purchasable from the stands for about a dollar and a half and is usually read by people that have some plans for building. It is a book that is usually kept for a year as against the magazine issue, which is usually not kept. The same house, at one time, was scheduled for a Better Homes and Gardens issue that was to be entitled, Fifty Best Homes Across the Nation. The editor, Red Seney, after some considerations decided that between the Idea Book issue and the Home section publication, that it was getting a little too much publicity; not new, etc. Also, time was running short for the issue. Also there will soon be published an article on me released to the newspapers in the area about the award that was presented to me by the Southern California Edison Company for outstanding electrical design in homes. It is undoubtedly a publicity gimmick for the S. Calif. Ed. Co. I guess, but it won't hurt me either.

I am doing an $185,000.00 Recreation Center (for the

Point Dume Mobile-home Park for the Adamson Company) all by myself. I can't find competent help since the upswing in building activity and I will not put on inferior people. I tried it once and very nearly had to pay for some of his errors myself. This is not good for business. I have two or three clients waiting and have just put them off until I can get some time in February.

I have three interesting houses under construction. One is a thirty-three hundred square foot house on the beach with caissons jack-hammered into solid rock fourteen feet below sand level and five feet below water level. We're sure learning a lot on this one. That's the Doerner job.

Mike Bright, my Olympic volleyball champion client and surfboard fiberglass client (He's the one that made our boards) and I decided to chuck it all today and we went surfing at the Colony Break (below the house here) for an hour. It was great fun and a great tension reliever. He gave me a wet-suit top, free. So, now I'm in good shape for the fifty-four-degree water. I used up seventy gallons of our seventy-five-gallon water heater trying to thaw out when I got home.

The rainstorms have been severe but no damage has been done to our place or anyone we know with the exception of a few minor leaks. I would really enjoy the storms except that I had one house framed up without the roof on. It got caught in a pretty bad stage. By the way, your letter came and we really enjoyed it. We are looking forward to your trip out here. Much Love, Doug.

COMMENTS

I don't remember doing a dozen jobs in 1968, but since building takes almost a year perhaps I might have been dealing with a dozen at one stage or another in one year. I got my award from the Edison Company, but it seemed nothing special, and yes, I picked up a job from the Adamson

Company for whom I'd been a consultant for four years. Anson Philips was general manager, Jeanie, secretary, and principals, Rhoda May Adamson Dallas, Merritt Adamson and Sylvia Adamson-Neville. This job was a major plus for my business and helped me bring in a reasonable income. I remember the Bright job and the Larson house in Topanga were all in process in 1968. Then, in the fall of 1968 Dick Gross arrived before dawn to take photographs of the pedestal house. He said the wait for publication usually seemed interminable, but now it is guaranteed to happen on February 9th, 1969.

ADVENT OF MONEY

There were good things happening at the beginning of 1969. The year before I had made a profit and paid down some of our second trust deed to *the father of our house,* Gus Konz. Our middle daughter Lilianne had been pleading with us for months to learn the piano. We acquired an inexpensive one for $200.00 and placed it downstairs in the entry near the circular stairway and she began lessons with Mrs. Chayes in Pacific Palisades. We also used it for rehearsals of the Neo Renaissance Singer's.

We were desperately desirous of filling our wonderful house with contemporary furniture, art, and compatible accessories. In 1969 an architect could buy furniture for 40% under list price. That was a little over wholesale. We were happy to take advantage of this special offer and bought a fine Dux sofa, two Dux lounge chairs, a Hans Wegner dining room set, a Hans Wegner bar cabinet and two classic Aero Saarinen pedestal side tables. These new pieces along with our Hans Wegner sewing cabinet given me for back wages by a former architect who owed me drafting money allowed us to approach our American dream.

We even bought a bronze bird-on-the-wing sculpture a foot-or-so high for seven hundred dollars. The artist was the resident professor of sculpture at the University of Buenos Aires in Argentina. For a few months he was showing and selling his work in the United States. As afore mentioned, we acquired Dick Haines oil painting called *The Peasant Girl*. It was intended as a companion piece to *The Gospel Singers* also painted by Dick. Harry Heckendorf built us bookshelves in our living room made of vertical grain Douglas Fir stair treads. We filled them with an increasing number of books and filled our house with Karon's miscellaneous works, papier-mâché butterflies, weavings, and my own artistic attempts. With the family's interest in surfing, swimming, and playground sports and with our *floating-in-air* sophisticated house, we made significant strides toward creating what we thought to be the cultured family home of artists, musicians and philosophers.

CONTEXT

In 1969 in America and Southern California, things happening in the world blow the mind! I refer to activities chronicled in two books to which I am particularly indebted. The first is *The Timetables of American History*, edited by Lawrence Urdang, and National Geographic's, *Eyewitness to the 20th Century*.

My life, my family's life, my friend's, client's, and colleague's life, in fact the lives of everyone in the world, are simultaneously played out against the background of change. Looking back, changes seem adventures of another age. In 1969 Neil Armstrong and Buzz Aldrin did nothing less than step on the surface of the *moon*. Neil said, *"That's one small step for man, one giant leap for mankind."* Judy Garland was found dead at 47 in London. The Manson family killed six people, including Roman Polanski's pregnant wife, Sharon Tate. Edward Kennedy's career was marred when his car plummeted into a pond

A Tale of Two Houses

on Chappaquiddick Island drowning Mary Jo Kopechne. Instead of regular security guards, the Rolling Stones hired the Hell's Angels, *for control of drugs, love and rock-and-roll* at Woodstock. A new American Football League *(AFL)* quarterback, Joe Namath, led the New York Jets to victory defeating winners of the National Football League, *(NFL)* Baltimore Colts. Players were paid *$15,000.00.* Thereafter the contest was called *The Super Bowl.* Yasar Arafat took over the Palestine Liberation Organization. Bert Bachrach composed *Raindrops Keep Fallin' On My Head,* a theme used in the film, *Butch Cassidy and the Sundance Kid,* with Paul Newman and Robert Redford. Boeing produced the *747 jet* passenger plane, and the French made final tests on the first supersonic *Concorde.* Television introduced Sesame Street. Woody Allen produced the film, *Take the Money and Run.* Thor Heyerdahl set off around the world floating in a papyrus-reed raft.

HOME SECTION

I was nevertheless waiting for my own drama to unfold. The sun was to dawn for me on February 9, 1969. I was to be publicized in the Sunday edition of the Los Angeles Times on the cover of Home magazine. It began with headlines:

> *An architect's*
> *own home,*
> *placed on a*
> *pedestal for*
> *a better look*
> *at the world*
> *around it.*

Inside were six glorious color pages plus a half-column of text on page 24.

84   Trial By Fire - *Doug Rucker*

Another quote:

> *We never knew
> there was so much
> going on…until
> we moved up here.*

29. Cover of HOME section, February 9, 1969.

A Tale of Two Houses

Dan McMasters wrote the article, a portion of which follows:

"The most striking thing about this striking house, says the man that lives there, is something you don't even see. It's a sort of an expanded consciousness that comes from living in it."

30. House from below taken with wide-angle lens - to be more dramatic says Dick Gross, photographer.

I loved to read what others were to say about my work and me. I felt important; like I was doing something creative that had public appeal; that perhaps the new dramatic house would bring about a change in my practice; that I might henceforth be doing significant Southern California architecture like my elder peers, Thornton Abell, Quincy

Jones, Craig Ellwood, John Lautner, Killingsworth, Brady and Smith, Buff, Straub & Hensman, Gordon Drake, etc. The publication filled me with hope.

Another quote, *"Douglas Rucker is that man, an architect who designed it for his family (Not true, of course. I designed it as a spec house for Gordon and I to sell.) He becomes almost incandescent as he talks about the house."* (Incandescent?)

"The story is the view and what it does to you. We never knew there was so much going on in the world until we moved up here. We see skydivers jumping from a plane 11,000 feet up, falling free for half that distance and landing on a target on the Malibu strand. We look down into the brush and see rabbits and quail and sometimes deer. We watch the rains go storming over the sea and clouds come billowing up. Just to the east the Serra Retreat sits on a hilltop and sometimes at sunset on a rainy day it will be perfectly framed by a rainbow. And when there's a storm in

31. Karon setting table. Artwork by Richard Haines.

the mountains, we'll see 60 foot trees and boulders big as a piano come churning down the Arroyo to the sea."

"On some weekends there will be sixty sailboats there, and always there are surfers catching the best 'breaks' on this whole coast. The fog never comes twice the same way, and sometimes it fills the valley until it stretches away like a floor from all sides of our deck. On a moonlight night the geranium gardens on the flatland below glow as with a soft fire…"

32. Interior of house looking east.

"You reach the upper level of the Douglas Rucker house by a spiral stair in the stairwell shown at the left of the facing page. There is a skylight above, and on the walls is displayed the art produced or collected by the family. The large work is a cartoon for a mural and was done by Richard Haines, who also did the portrait above the sofa in the living room."

"Doug Rucker is an architect who keeps telling himself he ought to work a nine-to-five day like normal people. But because he is a one-man office, and because he is a stickler for detail and loves to experiment, he often finds himself working twelve hours a day, and on weekends because

he is his own boss and because he catches fire with such projects as playhouse for his girls, he may go two or three

33. Interior of central stair hall showing top of circular stair and Dick Haines cartoon for mural, The Gospel Singers.

days with no work at all. And all of this is part of the reason why this home of his in Malibu is so personal and so fascinating ..."

"He might not have kept going if it had not been for his builder, Gordon Ewert. Mortally ill at the time, Ewert channeled all his energies and enthusiasm into fulfilling this design. 'To him it was the most beautiful thing he had ever done.' Rucker says.' He lived for it. He bragged about it. How could I let him down?"

"There are five Ruckers - Doug, his wife, Karon, and three daughters, aged 8, 6, and 10. There is also a dog and two Siamese cats. None has fallen off the deck yet, though Rucker doesn't take that hazard lightly. The distance from the deck to the ground on the downhill side is some 32 feet..."

"'If I'd built the house on the ground, I'd have had to burrow into the hill until it looked like a bunker. I'd have lost the view on two sides and cars would have parked on the roof so that area would have been lost, too'. Instead I developed a sort of pedestal with six [sic] columns of steel sunk in concrete caissons. On this frame I then placed the steel beams - the way a waiters fingers balance a tray - and on these beams I built a standard post and beam house. This gives a view from every side, and the structure has a dynamic look that brings it alive."

The Los Angeles Times Home section publication was the best exposure I'd ever had. The house was unusual and friends and relatives to whom I'd sent the article were congratulatory and happy for me. The world did not stop, though and I was in the midst of plenty to do with the Adamson Company's Mobile Home Recreation Complex. I launched into it with added zest, still riding my publication peak.

SINGING

The Sixth Annual Festival of the Music of Johan Sebastian Bach was to be performed by the Wilton Chamber Ensemble and the Neo Renaissance Singers. It was probably given in the Presbyterian Church on the 12th and 13th of April, 1969. On the first night the Chamber Orchestra was to play the Brandenberg Concerto #1 in F. Our neighborhood friend, Phoebe Liebig, contralto and member of the Singers, sang a Cantata solo prior to the Wilton Chamber Ensemble accompanying the Renaissance Singers in the Coffee Cantata by Bach. Karon Rucker was to sing soprano, William Gleason, bass, and Robert Faris, tenor.

Our motion-picture, historian, architect, *renaissance man*, Bill Gleason, had a wonderfully deep voice and loved the classics. He hadn't sung publicly for at least ten years, but was pleased to be asked to sing bass in a Bach trio with Karon and Renaissance Singer's director, Bob Faris. Bill was understandably concerned about his part, hired a tutor and *memorized* his part in two weeks. On performance night, watching the three standing in the spotlight, I noticed Bill, who was well over six-feet-tall and towered over Bob Faris at five-feet-six inches and Karon at five-feet-three inches. Karon and Bob, also a regular tenor with the Roger Wagner Choral, read music from their notebooks. I had to admire tall Bill with his remarkable stage presence when he faced the audience squarely and sang his part from memory without a mistake.

A week later the entire chorus and soloists of the Neo Renaissance Singers concluded with a Cantata, two concertos and Bach's Cantata, the Wachet Auf. I was never a soloist and if I wasn't on pitch I purposely waited for a colleague to introduce the note so I could follow. I didn't want to spoil the music and considered it my job to add little crescendos and stop singing altogether during pianissimos. Though I loved the music, I probably never would have joined

A Tale of Two Houses

the Singers if it weren't so important to Karon. Nevertheless, I had a 12-year chorus experience I wouldn't trade.

EVENING OUTLOOK

On May 9th, 1969 the Santa Monica *Evening Outlook* published pictures and an article on the American Institute of Architect's Malibu Home Tour to be held May 18, 1969. It included a photo of the interior of our living room and a distance shot of our house against the Malibu Mountains. The exterior of the Fred Lyman's house was also shown. It was entitled:

VIEW HOMES ARE UNIQUE

"Two of the homes singled out for the May 18 Home Tour of the Southern California Chapter of the American Institute of Architects and the Women's Architectural League are personal statements by the architects who designed them and now own them."

"The homes belong to Douglas W. Rucker, AIA, and Frederic P. Lyman, AIA. The Rucker home was created to house a family and it can still be enlarged through the addition of a third "floor" underneath the two existing floors. The Lyman structure, on the other hand, was designed as a bachelor's pad (and was featured by Playboy Magazine as the Airy Aerie), and is now the architect-owners studio."

"Both buildings are hillside dwellings, commanding sweeping views of the mountains and sea, and both stand exposed to the elements. In each case the architect took full advantage of the view and came up with a unique design to cope with the problems of such a hillside site."

"Overlooking the sea, Malibu Colony, fields of blooming geraniums, Serra Retreat, Malibu Creek and Santa Monica Mountains, the Rucker house is supported on a steep mountainside by a 35-foot pedestal and is cantilevered 17 feet in all directions."

"A crafts room, architect's studio and entrance hall are on the first level with the garage. (Carport) A spiral oak (steel and oak) staircase leads to an art gallery on the second level, around which are grouped the living and dining areas, two children's rooms, two baths, the master bedroom and a sewing room."

The pictures and commentary took up a third of a newspaper page opposite the sports section and an equal space was in praise of Fred's unique design.

"Lyman's bachelor pad turned studio is constructed like a giant piece of furniture, with redwood columns anchored by steel plates. Floor-to-ceiling windows look out on the sea and mountains. The first level boasts a copper fireplace at one end of the room for bachelor cooking. A desk and bookcases line the rear wall. Upstairs, via an outdoor staircase, where the bachelor owner slept under the stars - after the canvas roof was rolled back - are tables and files and drawing boards. Two of Lyman's assistants are hard at work at the drawing boards, and the canvas roof is drawn tightly closed. Lyman and his wife and children live elsewhere"

Fred was a close friend and previously had shared office space over the Malibu Country Store with architect Barry Gittleson and a now well-known female architect and writer, Cory Buckner. I loved Lyman's house. It is built entirely of redwood derived from ancient Japanese timber construction. Fred used no nails, but connected beam-to-girder-to-post with driven wedges and used hardwood pegs for bolts and fasteners. To visit Fred's house was to see how an American could utilize ancient and classic details of oriental architecture for Southern California.

A Tale of Two Houses

TOUR PREPARATION

Prior to being allowed to participate in the show, the AIA informed me I'd have to be a Chapter Member. I paid my dues and joined. It was a supreme compliment for our house to be selected by the AIA for its expensive and highly publicized Home Tour of 1969. I would now be recognized; not only as a competent Malibu architect, but one who was also creative, inspired, and could produce a reasonable construction on a difficult site. The pedestal house was dramatic and an architect's dream. Who would *not* like to be favorably recognized, even lauded, by his architectural peers? This was the AIA! This was the American Institute of Architects who had selected my house as one of five in the Malibu area to be acclaimed and publicly displayed.

Thinking now, I would never have gotten into this position had not strange and unplanned circumstances fallen into place. At the center of destiny were Gordon Ewert, Gus Konz and favorable lending conditions. Good luck that Gordon and I had met Gus who was willing to sell us the property for $8,500.00, a subordination clause, and three years to pay. Good luck Gordon and I leapt at the opportunity and Gordon showed me *I* was in control over *my* life in architectural designs. It was he, like a loving brother, who encouraged me and egged me on. Good luck, my neighbor in the housecoat argued with and shook her finger at Glendale Federal's lending official who was provoked into a rebellious mood and gave us a loan. Good luck, my friends and professionals, Harry Heckendorf and John Diefenderfer, were available as carpenter-contractors. Bad luck for Gordon *(and those who loved him)* when he died of brain cancer. Good luck that Karon agreed to make the pedestal house our own and move to Malibu. Good luck, the location and strange shape of the site required a unique pedestal design that could be seen by all of Malibu. Except for Gordon's death, I am thankful for favorable instances and recognize them from a human standpoint as *pure good luck!*

Before the house was to be on exhibition, Karon and I worked hard to get it and the property in condition for showing. We wanted the house to be artistic and cultured as we thought ourselves to be and have dignity, meaning and authority. Late in 1968, though it seemed a two-edged sword for Karon, I was delighted when I heard the news of the forthcoming tour. Being a mother in the PTA, soloist in a choral group, pursuing weaving activities, teaching swimming, participating in a Malibu social life, and other interests that seemed to me almost compulsive, she had little time to work in whatever form for additional aggrandizement. Inwardly I suppose Karon was pleased; however her messages to me were unclear and again, never verbalized. Then too, as I suspect for any woman, she considered the house her intimate space, her private dwelling to which she could return from the bustle of the outside world to rest and conduct her confidential business. In one respect she viewed the Tour as an invasion of privacy. It would not be cheap in emotions, time or money.

It was not that I disagreed with her, but I was ready to do everything necessary to be included on the AIA tour. My ego and desire for business and approval longed for satisfaction. My dreams about what this could mean to my future practice, my idea that I'd henceforth do stunning, contemporary work, and it appealed to me to be admired and sought after. If I had work, I'd have more money and my family could live an easier life. For me the house *was* an architect's dream.

We painted the walls, stained the woodwork and washed the windows. We dusted, bought new slipcovers, displayed new artwork, polished floors, cleared brush and removed superfluous toys and debris. We scrubbed and polished the parquet floors, removed cars, hosed down the motor court, and strategically placed new, healthy large-leafed potted plants on the motor court and decks to give the appearance of a cared-for house, dignified, cultured and aware. We wanted the house to demonstrate our family as *together*.

HOME TOUR

It was a wonderful day, not a cloud in the sky, the sun, brilliant with a sharp horizon and the slim line of Catalina protruding slightly above a low-lying mist. I wore a pair of slacks, open collared shirt and suave-looking shoes over tan socks. Karon was showered and coiffed with a hint of lipstick and clothing befitting her self-concept - artistic and avant-garde. We felt ourselves and our home was seen at its best.

(It is probable that Viveka (9), Lilianne (just 7) and Amanda (5), were absent for the tour. I don't remember them there, nor does Viveka remember attending. I can't imagine shepherding three children through a crowd of so many. Normally Karon's mother, Lois, would have been on hand, but at tour-time she and Duke were living in Mountain Home, Arkansas.)

Attractive members of the Women's Architectural League, usually married to young architects, arrived an hour before our guests at 9:00 AM. With yellow ribbon they cordoned off the master bedroom, children's rooms, sewing room, and portions of the living and dining rooms. Several smartly dressed young ladies stationed themselves upstairs and downstairs to welcome guests, point the way, and answer questions. They were willing representatives for the proper and correct exhibition of a special house on an expensive, dignified tour. Guests would be allowed on the circular stairway and directed upstairs to the skylight and art foyer. They would be permitted to pass freely between the living room and dining room to the surrounding deck and walk around the deck to observe the view. From the deck the guests could also look into the house through the screened, open, sliding glass doors and see each room in the house. The public could use the downstairs powder room as necessary. My downstairs office around the circular stairway was free territory for everyone to explore.

About noon I stood just inside the sliding glass door in the conference section of my tiny office. I was on the motor court level, watching people come and go on our driveway. Visitors who had parked on the street could be seen walking carefully down our steep driveway, pausing, now and then, to marvel at the view. Those who were leaving accepted their fate and trudged courageously up, acknowledging those descending and stopped frequently to catch their breath.

Occasionally an elderly person, unable to traverse the steep driveway, would be driven down and up in a small car. Guards with walkie-talkies were located along the drive to prevent walking visitors from being hit by the car. Arriving guests sometimes examined views from the motor court before entering the house. When visitors reached the front door they were greeted by a young woman from the Architectural League and invited to enter and enjoy themselves. The circular stairs and the skylight that could be seen from below were an invitation to see the art gallery at the top of the stairs and to experience the loftier house and deck views.

Still in my conference area about noon I found myself standing next to a dark, well-dressed, good-looking young man. When he saw someone he knew he seemed pleased to introduce me as the architect. His friends shook hands with me and were always complementary. I enjoyed being fussed over like it was my birthday and when time permitted, I apologized to the handsome young man and asked to whom I was speaking? *"Robert Bolling,"* he answered.

I inquired about his profession. *"I'm an architect,"* he

said. Enthused to meet a fellow professional, I asked if he was an AIA member. *"Yes!"* I told him I was too. I said I'd just joined so I could be on the AIA tour and asked how long he'd been a member. With a shy smile he said, *"About ten years. I'm President."* I was embarrassed. I was a member who'd never gone to a meeting. I had not read the *Building News* in which Robert Bolling had a weekly column. I liked him immediately and thought to myself, *here's the President of the AIA helping exhibit my house.* I was flattered, but I kept my thoughts to myself.

Eventually over two hundred people braved their way up and down our steep driveway to see our house. The last of the guests departed about 6:00 PM. The Women's League stayed to clean up and left our house picked up and Karon and I alone and exhausted.

The following week was anti-climactic. We appreciated the rewards of a clean, brush-cleared house and our lovely new furniture purchases. We rested on the laurels of the previous months work and quickly accustomed ourselves to an improved life style.

NINE DAYS RAIN

*L*ater in the year Malibu had heavy rains. It rained straight for nine days and ten nights with no let-up. It didn't rain lightly but came on either strong or in torrents. It beat against our windows and trailed in streams off our eaves and decks to form erosive channels on the hillside leading to wider tributaries. With wind driving the rain uphill, we were drenched from below as well as from above. The one thing it *did* do was rain *continuously*, all day, all night, moment-to-moment, hour-to-hour, for nine long days. The media called it the *Pineapple Express,* a continuous flow of rain-laden clouds blowing across the Pacific from the direction of Hawaii and dropping moisture to give Southern California a complete soaking. We were getting a rain-test.

To quote from my usual reference book for 1969, *"Rains in California caused mudslides that destroyed or damaged 10,000 homes and killed 100."* It was gloomy. It was hard to work. It dampened spirits. The canyons were closed. We couldn't drive. Construction stopped.

During the first three days the ground became saturated and Malibu Creek thickened and began its heavy flow, rumbling toward the ocean. On the third day, up and down the coast, swirls of sediment-laden water curled in brown, dirty hoops a quarter mile off shore. The ocean looked invaded, worried, and unhappy with itself.

While trying to sleep on the sixth night Karon and I were disconcerted when we heard an unfamiliar throaty roar rising from Malibu Creek. The eerie sound penetrated the whole estuary and was caused by huge boulders one to four feet in diameter on their forced trip downstream clacking and grunting over one another. This continued each night and for the remainder of the rain. The sandy strip that usually separated the lagoon from the ocean had long since been penetrated and a wide, dirty stream of river-water had forced its way through the barrier, invading the ocean.

Our close friends, the Resnick's, were severely threatened by the nine-day rainstorm. They were living in a beautifully designed house they'd built deep in the bottom of the Malibu Creek flood plain. One early morning in a spirit of concern I bicycled across the bridge and through the Serra Retreat to see how they were doing. When I reached their house, I was shocked to discover the raging Malibu Creek had opened a new channel parallel to the main watercourse. The water had cut a wide channel through the Resnick's driveway and their house was now on a narrow island sandwiched between two dangerous currents. The creek had forked apart and back together again at either end of the house. The Resnick's were marooned on a gravelly strip of dirt with a magnificent house, a pool, and a few trees.

In an attempt to help the family escape, firemen had

A Tale of Two Houses

already arrived and braving the rain had shot a line across the new channel. Bernie Resnick and the firemen attached it to trees on either side and pulled it tight. Then firemen strapped to a safety harness and pulley, with feet and shins sometimes dragging, crossed the current on the cable and labored each family member thirty-feet-or-so to safety. They returned for the next person and so on until everyone was safe. I believe Bernie stayed on the island to sandbag, shovel, waterproof and do what he could to save his house.

The house was not washed away. Bernie, Rheta and their family survived to live another day. Cleanup was costly and horrendous. Learning from this almost fatal experience, Bernie immediately built retaining walls sufficient to keep future floodwaters from opening a similar channel. I'm sure it was an adventure the Resnick's will never forget. I haven't forgotten.

34. Dissipation of the Pineapple Express.

After nine days the *Pineapple Express* dissipated and the welcome sun came out. Inspecting the Malibu Creek bridge one day I spotted seven or eight huge Sycamore trees sixty to ninety-feet long and two to three-feet in diameter lying upstream and distributed randomly through the lagoon. They had been uprooted in the rainstorm, slid into Malibu Creek, and had been carried downstream to land where fate decreed. In the still raging creek and widened lagoon they lay stiff and dead, water swirling and pooling around their extended branches. The flattened tree trunks remained permanent in the gravely bottom for years afterward. Eventually they became bald and bare and adventurous children climbed over them and rode them like horses.

Though Malibu's topsoil dried quickly, rainwater continued to penetrate the hills and sink deeply beneath the surface. It replenished the water table. With latent seepage into the depths of the dirt, hillsides became more thoroughly saturated and slides were triggered. The first was along Pacific Coast Highway. Others followed in Malibu Canyon, Tuna Canyon, Topanga Canyon, Latigo, and Coral Canyons. Huge boulders slipped from mountainsides and rolled across the highways to fall deeper into the canyon. They left a sloping pile of mud and sediment that blocked traffic. Occupants might have been crushed were they caught beneath certain slides.

When the bridge at Las Flores Canyon became blocked with logs, boulders and sandy dirt, long streams of mud spilled over Pacific Coast Highway and rushed into garages and beach houses to run dripping down stairways to the beach and carried out to sea by strong ocean currents. On the Malibu shoreline in places where beach sand had been eroded up to twelve feet, pilings hung in the air. In many cases the apartments and houses fell out of plumb and sagged depressingly. I'd known about Malibu fires. This time I got to see Malibu's other face, rains and slides.

AFTER THE HOME TOUR

When things settled down after the tour I was having fun and being challenged by doing all the working drawings all by myself on the Adamson Company's Recreation Complex. To keep me abreast and informed, I had weekly meetings with the Adamson Company's Bob Finley and Anson Philips. Bob Finley, a talented engineer, brought humor, energy and experience to his job. Anson Philips, the man in front and sometimes symbol of the Adamson Company, was their manager. He worked for many years directly under Merritt, Rhoda Mae and Sylvia Adamson Neville. With Bob and Anson's help I eventually guided the Recreation Complex through the County permit process and in early September 1969 we began grading.

Charlie Decker's firm was doing the grading work. This was the time when the old bulldog working-man's-working-man made his memorable comment to Bob and me. Chatting alongside a chugging dozer in the middle of an immense graded plateau, the discussion turned to accuracy in grading. Tanned face with eyes in a slit beneath the shadow of his hat and dead-serious, Charlie took the cigar out of his mouth and growled, *"I can grade forty acres within an eighth of an inch,"* and held up his forefinger and thumb with the cigar to show how big an eighth of an inch was. Bob Finley and I stood there in the hot sun. We looked at each other and couldn't think of a comment. Who were we not to believe?

BUILDING NEWS

Architectural life persisted through 1969 with construction of the Recreation Complex and the Anderson, Doerner, Davis and Bright houses. The normal Rucker family persisted as well with the children reaching ages five, seven, and nine. In December I received a publication of the Building News and a full page spread of our house. The news again assuaged my enormous ego.

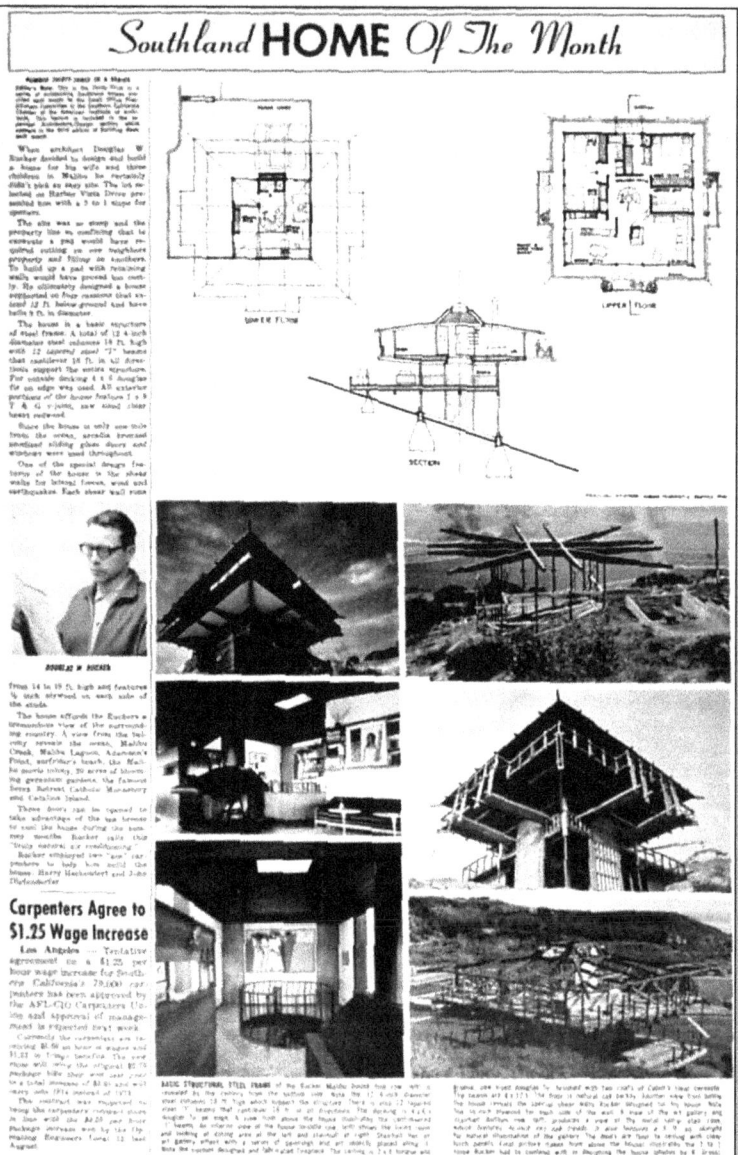

35. Southland Home of the Month. Building News 12-19-1969.

CHILDREN'S LIFE

While the Recreation Complex was finishing we went through the standard Christmas and New Years for 1969. Recently I ran across an Easter Card from Mother's file drawn by Lilianne and sent to her *Gramma* in Golden, Colorado.

36. Girl with flowers. (Back side of typed and illustrated Easter card to Rucker grandparents by Lili Rucker.)

And also from Mother's files a note written by six-year-old Amanda:

Letter - No Date
Dear Granma,
    I am on my bed crying in pain because I fell down the stairs outside and sprained b y ainkel. (I don't know how to spell that word yet so this. (drawing of foot) my foot is swollen and it really herts & I can't walk on it without it herting badly. I tried to tell granny but she got mad aout something and wouldn't listen.
    I want Dad to look at it tomarow morning. It's righ in between (drawing of foot with arrow pointing to front of ankle labeled, hear.) and it doesn't hert in back right (same drawing of foot with arrow pointing) hear.
    I hope it isn't a brake and it heals by tomarow.
Love Mandy
P. S. Do you think it could be a brake?

HAL ROSSON

During the years 1966 to 1970 Bill Gleason had entertained us at our home sporadically bringing his 16-millimeter projector with reels of classic film he rented or borrowed from the studios. On certain evenings our group of twelve to sixteen friends would be perched in our pedestal house overlooking the restless string of lights moving along the Coast Highway with the vast ocean disappearing into the night. We served wine, coffee, and desert while Bill showed movies like the definitive *Robin Hood* with Errol Flynn, Olivia de Haviland, Claude Rains and Basil Rathbone, or *Key Largo* with Humphrey Bogart, Lauren Bacall, Edward G. Robinson, Claire Trevor, and Lionel Barrymore.

One evening Bill announced he would be bringing over a close friend, Hal Rosson. Hal was an elderly cinematographer who had won the Academy Award for filming the 1946 production of *The Wizard of Oz*. He also photographed over fifty films including *Red Dust* ('32), *Captain's Courageous* ('37), *Duel in the Sun* ('50), and *Sing'n in the Rain* ('50). Rosson had a short-term marriage to Jean Harlow whose career was tragically cut short when she died from kidney failure at the age of twenty-six.

Having an award-winning cinematographer who photographed the film, Red Dust, thirty-eight years ago, was an unexpected pleasure. His attendance marked the beginning of a pleasant and lasting relationship between Hal and our family.

Hal later bought a house I had designed for the Dorr family on a bluff overlooking the beautiful blue Pacific. It had been constructed of clear heart redwood and in size was well over 4,000 square-feet. Hal lived there with an oriental man's-servant for a year or two, but when he decided to sell it, he offered it to our family for $425,000.00, a steal in 1971. We declined and it was purchased instead by comedy actor Henry Gibson and his wife.

Letter – No Date
Dear Mother and Dad,
"I'm really emotionally ready to retire. (I was 41) If I did retire, I would still work. By retiring, I actually mean being financially independent and having time to do the architectural works that really grab me. I would also throw pots, sculpt, paint, study music, write songs, poetry & stories, practice springboard diving, surf, run, work out on the trampoline, etc. Financial independence would mean that I would just do everything slower, having more time, and in the long-run do less than if I were pressed for time. There is some kind of law that says if you have more time to do something, you will use up all that time doing it."

Then again:

"I went to the library and withdrew five books, two on Giotto, the 16th century painter, one on hypnotism, one on voice and singing, and one entitled On Growing Older. In the Growing Older book, Paul Dudley, MD, who was President Eisenhower's doctor says:

"Now as to the program for the aged themselves, in the first place, it must be individualized in every case; secondly, it must air at all three sides of man, physical, mental, and spiritual; and thirdly, it must be recognized by everyone that the brain is man's most important organ and must have an optimal circulation of blood. An essential way to secure such an optimal circulation is to keep the leg muscles vigorously moving. There are several reasons for this: they are the biggest muscles of the body. In their contraction, they squeeze the veins which are armed with valves, and the blood can flow in only one direction, and that is up against gravity. Muscular fatigue due to exercise is undoubtedly the best tranquilizer and antidote for stress that man possesses. And finally, there is increasingly clear evidence now that in

some biochemical way, active muscular metabolism retards the development of a serious disease of the intimae of the arteries called arteriosclerosis, which obstructs the blood flow to the heart, the brain, and other important parts of the body. Nearly everyone can walk at any age, and this is probably the simplest of all routine exercises to recommend, abandoning the automobile except for essential needs."

I had no idea on May 7th, 1970 that I was to adopt the forgoing quotation as my own philosophic foundation for despite my new interest in wine I was soon to begin an unbroken, long-standing running program.

WINE AND FLU

To be like others thus gaining *maturity* and justifying the action as a before dinner appetizer, I'd begun opening a bottle of cooled, inexpensive wine to join Karon for a glass before dinner. We, or at least I, had another glass or two during dinner, then after dinner the remainder had to be finished, which I dutifully did before putting the kids to bed. It was my habit to read them a story, or more conveniently, make up a story and tell them about the buzzard and the monkey. After that and the wine having had time to settle, I'd feel logy, unambitious and slightly sick to the stomach. Over the year or year-and-a-half of habitual drinking I'd gained weight and was now up to 172 pounds. This, for me on a five foot-seven inch frame, was heavy. I didn't feel drunk after a half or two-thirds of a bottle of wine or particularly relaxed. I didn't think I was an alcoholic because three glasses of wine daily *does not a drunk make. (Or does it?)* Indeed, Doctor's say for the health of the elderly, one glass of red wine with dinner is actually *recommended*. However the alcoholic personality *does* attain an uncontrollable habit. Did I have a habit? Was I a borderline alcoholic? Wine went down easily, but made me slightly sick afterward. Was the *slightly sick* a side-affect of the price of *maturity*?

That same year, 1969, was the year of the Hong Kong flu. At any event I got it and threw-up for almost a week. Then I became feverish and weak and went to bed with an extreme loss of appetite and feeling at times in mortal danger. Three weeks of care by Karon and sometimes her mother, Lois, finally brought me to the point where I was hungry. I'd lost twelve pounds and weighed a hundred-sixty. A few more days elapsed and feeling better with a reasonable breakfast like bacon, eggs, orange juice, toast, and coffee, I was surprised to find out I actually felt *good*. I'd been off wine and on a forced fast for three weeks. I had lost twelve pounds and my blood pressure was no longer high. My heart, instead of pounding stiff and noisily in my chest, was comfortably quiet and for the first time since I'd moved into the house, I had a weird sensation of calm.

In light of my weight loss and feeling calm, I decided to quit wine. The next morning I took a partially empty bottle and two full bottles of wine and ceremoniously poured the contents down the sink. I watched the purple and yellow stuff disappear down the little hole into eternity and told Karon I was hereinafter off wine. Wine was not *me!* I would drink wine no longer! Karon didn't argue with my decision.

RUNNING

Shortly thereafter, I don't know how I got there, but I found myself walking across the Malibu Creek Bridge feeling the breeze and enjoying the canyon view. I noticed the creek was wide and shallow. The water was dark and clear disappearing slowly and quietly under the bridge and meandering into the lagoon and ocean. Upstream it narrowed reflecting the sky until it lost itself in willow trees and green foliage. The sun was high and the outdoors was bright and fresh. I reflected on the simple fact that I used to like to run. Where had running gone? I hadn't run since college and that would be *twenty* years ago. In Chicago at

Austin High School I'd been on the football and track teams and at Illinois University I'd captained an intramural flag-football team for two seasons playing offense and defense. At the age of forty-two was I *past* the age of running? Was I too old to run? Was running *over*? Thinking myself out of condition on that sunny afternoon I broke into a slow trot and crossed the bridge to Cross Creek Road, then inland to Civic Center Way to the dirt road through Takahashi's geranium gardens and home. Though jogging slowly, I was surprised I could make it that far. I estimated my jog at three-quarters of a mile.

The idea of running had hit me. A week or so later I bought track shoes, the kind with removable steel spikes on leather soles with no heels, the kind for sprinting fast on the toes. I didn't know they were wrong for jogging and I didn't realize it, but I was making a life change. I'd given up drinking and lost twelve pounds. I felt good! Now with track shoes, shorts and tank-top I was ready for running. I went jogging in the mornings as often as I could. I jogged slowly and comfortably and at first ran only to the bridge and back. Then bit-by-bit I increased my distance past the bridge and ran along the sandy trails paralleling the Creek to the rolling Surfrider Beach sands. I rested for ten minutes watching the waves fold cleanly on the rocks and hiss and roll to the sandy shore. After a few months this habit allowed me to lose a few more pounds and I discovered I ate less, my lungs were aired out and my cardiovascular system was working better. I slept better, woke up earlier, and understood more of this special, natural gift of running. I became familiar with sun, sand, creek, and wave. I became more intimate with dirt, wildflowers, weeds, squirrels, rabbits, and coyotes. I ran through geranium gardens, past trees, clouds, wind, sun, fog, rain, Santana's and all the God-given, miraculous delights to be found outdoors in Southern California. Mentally, emotionally and physically, *jogging agreed with me!*

THOUGHTS ON MOVING

I had completed the *dream* house and had lived there for three years with all its pros and cons; long enough time to visualize it as our permanent home. Now that we were coming out of our financial difficulties, Karon and I had thoughts of moving. Paying the mortgage was a strain, but if it was our permanent home, some day we might be able to afford it. Moving had its disadvantages, it took courage to ascend our hazardous driveway several times a day. There was always fear that an accident might happen. Considering the height from which an out-of-control-car might fall, the accident would not be small. One slip of the brakes and we'd plummet to a crumpled death. We didn't take this lightly. There was little room on the decks for children to play and except for a small sandy yard beneath the house soon to be occupied by a trampoline, there was no flat space. When playing with friends on the decks an unwatched child could climb on a chair and fall thirty-five feet to the ground. It was tiring for us to limit the children's play and restrict their deck activities. The motor court, other than for cars, became the place for tricycles, wagons, skateboards, balls, dolls, dogs, cats and other pre-teen belongings. The motor court became the gathering place for children's play equipment and a perpetual obstacle course for cars arriving or backing.

Over time I'd begun to feel I'd achieved the glory and public relation benefits of the house and it might be time to move on. I'd hoped the house had appreciated in value. With a profit, perhaps I could choose another Malibu property on more level ground. I dreamt of designing us a new house compatible with our needs and reducing our living expenses.

At sporadic intervals over several months I found an almost flat piece of land a hundred feet square on a bluff between Broadbeach and Encinal Canyon Roads. Sandwiched between similar properties, it was off a private driveway that led directly to a private beach. Trees blocked the ocean view, but we'd be able to hear the breakers, smell the sea, and feel the cool westerly winds. The delight of the ocean, sand, and clear waters could readily be enjoyed. The price was reasonable, but before making an offer I made sketches that pleased me. The preliminary designs showed a perfectly square house with a double-pitched roof and rooms with floor to ceiling glass facing outside and radiating from a center entry. We continued to think about moving and with little fan-fare let it be known to a few real estate agents that the pedestal house was on the market. Our first house in Santa Monica Canyon was designed for speculation and our children were born there. The second house with Gordon and I as owners was also *not* designed for us, but meant for sale. This time we wanted a house designed exclusively for *us*.

SEPTEMBER 24, 1970

All people in the United States and Southern California had to get up and go to work against the background of local and world events previously mentioned. On a Malibu morning a fog probably crept to the windowsills of our pedestal house and it looked like the normal state of affairs for a September beach community - gloomy. No doubt I awakened Viveka and Lilianne for school before showering. They dressed and made their way to the breakfast counter for bowls of Cheerios and orange juice. While they were eating I made peanut butter and jelly sandwiches for school lunches and put them in brown paper bags with an apple and cookies. Sometimes I drew a happy-face on one side of their bags with a humorous comment on the other before giving them a nickel for milk and sending them off down the hill. Sometimes I drove them to school and raced up our driveway in my Volvo. *(I had to race up the hill. It was so steep, any car that didn't race up would stall and the passenger's lives would hang on the awareness of the driver and the quality of the*

A Tale of Two Houses

brakes.) Later in the day, before attending home-making and creative efforts, Karon would deliver Amanda to Mrs. Riggle at preschool at the Presbyterian Church

I was alone in my office. My former draftsman, Clyde, had left a few months earlier due to lack of work. I probably worked an hour on the board before donning a sweater, jumping in my Volvo, racing up the hill, and visiting a subcontractor at the Hillman addition. I probably answered a few questions and sketched a detail or two on the back of a spare 2"x4" board as an illustration.

In the afternoon I probably worked at my desk paying bills and writing letters before returning to my board and doing creative work on a new architectural job. While I drafted, I listened to classical music. Listening to classical music while drafting was and is a lifetime love. In the late afternoon the air was quiet and the office was still. The fog had evaporated and the weather seemed undecided. Perhaps we were in for a bit of a change.

Soon Viveka, Lilianne, and Amanda came home from school and found activities in their rooms upstairs, perhaps drawing or reading, or watching television black and white cartoons while lying on our bed in the master bedroom. During the day Karon did what mother's do, washing, ironing, writing letters, or working in her sewing room on her beloved weaving.

I'm sure we had a good supper, the five of us gathered around our dining table under our fixture made from an upside down teak waste paper basket. Viv, Lil, and Amanda probably told us of their school activities or mentioned a tidbit about their friends. After dinner while Karon washed the dishes I probably took the car to Ralph's Market, perhaps because Karon needed a half-gallon of milk, a jar of peanut butter or another loaf of bread. In those days the Mayfair Market was near the Malibu bridge on Cross Creek Road, its broad backside and the rear of other businesses paralleling the wide, slow-moving Malibu Creek. The stars were glorious when I left the house, but upon approaching the Mayfair, were obscured by business lights of the parking lot.

Mayfair Market was near the center of the wide Malibu estuary that contained many different environments within its broad alluvial fan. On a promontory was the Serra Retreat in a forest of eucalyptus trees, the vast expanse of geranium gardens, the well-lighted business district containing the Malibu Theater, Baskin-Robbins and the Mayfair, the bridge on Pacific Coast Highway and the swampy mouth of Malibu Creek. Between the lagoon and Surfrider Beach sat the historic Adamson's Beach House forever contemplating the idyllic rolling sand and rippling waves.

I parked in a semi-full lot and walked across the lot to the Mayfair, I sensed a soft wind skimming past my nose and ruffling my hair. It was blowing in the wrong direction - out to sea. Malibu normally has a westerly wind that sweeps across Point Dume and drives down the beach, but this breeze was warm and humid, drifting gently but persistently down the floors of Malibu Canyon Creek into its broad estuary toward the sea.

This warm and humid breeze was not *uncommon* coming from that direction. The desert winds, moving seaward through the steep walls of Malibu Canyon, gathered moisture and smells of vegetation. Not that I was worried, but to a person with experience, this marshy, canyon breeze with vaporous smells wafting through the steep crevice could only mean one thing - forerunners of a Santa Ana wind.

I got the milk, returned home, told my girls a story about the buzzard and the monkey, found out about Karon's day, went to bed, watched TV, and fell asleep.

PART 2
FIRE AND AFTERMATH

FIRE

On September 25, 1970, in Calabasas, ten miles inland on the ocean side of Ventura Freeway, a vicious, offshore wind combined with a flame no bigger than a small campfire whipped a blackening V through intervening mountains and the Malibu coast. The brush fire pounded through dry brush and hills to endanger a mountain community studded with live Oaks and Sycamores called Monte Nido. It was tucked around dry streams tributary to Malibu Creek just north of Malibu tunnel. Malibu fire trucks screamed inland down Malibu Canyon Road to aid the Calabasas Fire Department only to have the fire leapfrog over them heading for the ocean and blocking the slimmest hope of them returning to Malibu. Living in a pedestal house on an exposed promontory in the center of the mouth of Malibu Canyon, the Rucker family's fate was sealed.

Along with many other ill-fated homeowners including the huge, historic Serra Retreat Monastery, the pedestal house burned to the ground. Afterward, when things had calmed, I stayed up late in Bernie and Rheta Resnick's beautiful home in the Serra Retreat and several evenings after everyone had gone to bed, wrote a record to myself. I had to understand the sequence of events and determine what happened. We'd lost the house so quickly. It was hard to keep things straight. What happened first? What followed? Mentally, I tried to order the jumbled events. After digesting what I'd written, the thought came to me that other homeowners whose houses had burned could relate to my experience. Since Jim Toland and Dan McMasters had published my house in the Home section of the L. A. Times, they would remember it and might accept what I'd written as newsworthy. What follows is what I recorded and what the L. A. Times published, unedited. The Times named it:

DEATH OF A HOUSE.

The gray-brown column of smoke was again curling over our house. It was about 3:00 PM, an hour or so before everything we owned was to be destroyed by fire. Anxiety drove me to remove the brush pile I had so long been neglecting. Lilianne, 8, Mandy, 6, and Daisy, our "international" dog, were with me. Karon had taken a fast walk to the new library to meet Vivi, 10, coming home from school.

Lili helped Daddy, bringing trash barrels and asking if our house was going to burn down. I reassured her that we would be fine, that I was just taking precautions. "See," I said, "the smoke is blowing away from our house."

"If our house did burn down, where would we go?" Lili said.

"Grandma would be happy to have us."

We worked another 15 minutes and the smoke I "knew" to be at least six miles away in Calabasas (I had just heard a radio report) looked terribly close. But then, I knew that brush fire clouds could be deceiving. I'd seen and helped report the Latigo Canyon fire in Malibu two years before. The wind, hot and gusty, was rising a little now and the angry red sun was glaring through the clouds.

"Why is the sun so red, Daddy?" Asked Lili. I continued my clearing of the brush pile, jamming dry sumac branches into the trash barrels.

"Because the smoke is red."

Ashes were rising in the smoke coming over the hill and the clouds were definitely closer and admittedly huge. Tears formed dirty streaks on Lili's face and she began whimpering.

"Daddy, let's get away from here."

Mandy started crying, too, and said "Take us down to the library."

A hot blast of wind, dust, dry grass and a rolling tumbleweed brought more tears from both and I decided.

A Tale of Two Houses

"All right, I'll walk you down and you wait there with Vivi."

Though my gut was clutching now and then, I still felt I had time to walk the children down the hill to the library in the Malibu Civic Center a quarter-mile away, then return to my clearing and watering as precautionary measures only because, of course, the wind was still blowing westerly - away from the house.

Half way down our hill, an anxious child holding each hand and Daisy on a leash, I met Karon puffing up the hill. I told Lili and Mandy to run down the hill and wait for us with Vivi. We would pick them up shortly. Mandy, fearful, in tears, said "No, Daddy, you have to walk us down there." I finally gave her a single spank on the bottom that sent her running, crying after her sister and the dog. Hot gusts, flying grass and dust became definitely stronger as we returned to the house. Ashes, black and white, rose more clearly in the cloud rising over the hill.

Both Karon and I remembered what we had heard from those who had saved their homes two years earlier. "Those that stay with their homes during the fire will be able to save them." We believed those words but were understandably apprehensive since now it seemed remotely possible that it was soon to be us, not they, whose lives would be in jeopardy. We remembered, too, as we watered portions of our house, the stories of firemen pulling up their trucks and equipment, advancing as it were, with the speed of the fire to each successive home and saving it. Surely we would do our best and at the last minute, when the "chips were down," the professionals would pull us through. There would be smiles, thanks, admiration, and appreciation, even exhilaration at the marvelous job we had all done. Man against nature wins out after long battle, etc.

I went to my studio on the motor court level. The sky was dark with smoke. I flicked on a light ... nothing; another switch ... nothing. So, the power lines were down already. I'll keep silent, no need to panic Karon. Certainly the fire could not be so close as to already affect the power? Outside again, I continued my wetting down. I had held off watering because I didn't want to reduce the neighbor's pressure. If the fire did come our way the houses above us would need all they could get. It surely was our turn now and I really wasn't surprised at the lack of our water pressure. With two hoses running, nozzles turned for greatest throw, we averaged about six feet of spray, six inches if held against the wind. The feeling was one of futility. How could we soak a 1,600 square-foot house on a hillside with water pressure that would take a minute to fill a bucket? We did the best we could. Karon worked the motor court level. I worked below on the hillside. We shouted to one another over the wind that strengthened, came in long puffs, slacked off, came from the opposite direction. Then came that first gray-brown brush fire smoke sailing through, in and around our structure - filling our noses, smarting our eyes, filling us with dread. Appearing with the smoke was a young man who had walked up uphill from the highway, breathless, anxious; sure we were in danger but brave. He asked if we needed help. I handed him a hose.

More shouting of instructions, more work, more wind and worry, and our young helper, who'd had enough, cried that we had done all we could. "It's time to leave!" Our only helper. Though he was gone, I was not yet ready to go. Karon, too, kept right on working. There was so much soaking to be done and it went slowly because of the lack of pressure, and besides we were determined to "stay with the house." I finished below and joined my wife. I saw her in the heavy smoke shielding her mouth and eyes with something - intent on soaking everything, scared but determined, fighting for the nest and all our works.

It occurred to me to grab my wallet, for surely this was "it." But wouldn't I look silly running around in Levi's, T-shirt, gunboats, with a lumpy wallet bulging in my back pocket. Karon had stashed her purse just inside the entry door for

A Tale of Two Houses

a quick getaway. There was so much to do, so little time, so little water pressure. "We were "staying with it!"

I jumped in the black Volvo, screamed up the hill and parked it in a large brushed lot, then ran 400 feet back down the driveway and took up the sprinkling. The pine trees close by the house, bent double by the blasts of wind, reminded me of a nightmare I'd had many years ago in Chicago. It wouldn't be long until showdown time and I dreaded the fact that I was soon to see that huge, all-consuming monster climbing over and eating the ridge.

I drove the white Volvo station wagon 100 feet up the hill and parked it just past the row of pine trees along the driveway because intuition said if the pine trees burst into flame they would then not ignite the gas tank. I ran to the motor court, and it was from there I saw the lunatic flames on the far ridge, 1,000 feet or so away, careening this way and that, coloring and lighting the smoke, when at the same instant, the adjacent lot exploded into flame. We were hit far and near at the same instant. We had time and we had no time. Then impossibly stronger winds brought fire patches like bombs, which burst and grew and blackened and smoked all around us. The major "back-up" body of flame rolled directly toward us. It came up our draw with a fiercely red-black intensity. It came down the first ridge and was then, lost from sight behind the second ridge, then arose in terrible countenance over the next ridge. I saw the 100-foot alleppo pine that I had admired almost daily for four years ignite in a searing white flame. We were getting it all right. We kept to our watering as ashes and smoke stung our eyes. Some flying fire bombs had sailed past the house, struck and were now burning up toward us from the opposite side. As the fire came closer and the heat more intense, we decided, since the chips were down, we would soak or own clothing - soak ourselves. Into my mind came an image I had seen ten years earlier, of a burning man running through the night just after an auto accident in which a car, struck from behind, had literally blown up in the darkness, lighting the desert night sky for miles; this panicked man with all his clothes burning, running through the night.

We soaked our clothes. We'll see if the 200 feet of brush clearance will hold it's own. The heat was too intense and I stepped behind a glass wing-wall, looked down and saw that a ring of fire surrounded us. The brush was turning black behind the stationary, leading edge of flame. Perhaps we'll make it. The flames 10 feet high consumed, dropped to 6 feet high, ate up and dropped to 4 feet high. The clearance apparently was holding. The brush was turning black behind the fire. We worked at putting out several smaller fires from the other side of the house. The smoke clouds broke and a ray of true sunlight hit and illuminated the motor court. A breath of cool, true, fresh air in our nostrils. Somewhere there was a patch of blue sky. It occurred to me that, yes, "those who do stay with their homes..." We may make it. It's not so bad. Wow, stories I'll tell of how we almost lost the house. Doug and Karon, brave to the end, saved their house, "stayed with it." Keep cool, keep working, and put out fires.

These thoughts, like pearls, dropped into my aching head and even as I turned to shout the good news to Karon, the words were utterly lost in a blast of hot air, smoke and embers that shook the entire structure. And from another direction that much talked-about, 60 mile-an-hour fire storm blast hit us. A shower of hot embers from the now burned brush, by the thousands, flashed through and around us. In straight lines they came, like tracer bullets, pelting the windscreen, house, me, my lovely wife. A Fourth of July super-cone came flashing in sprays vertically between the railing and the court edge. No part of the house was spared from those flying embers. They went straight to every nook and cranny, even to the eaves and held by the stiff power of the winds, formed clusters like atoms, like tiny suns, and bored their way into our beautiful wood structure. Like acid *dropped on cheese, they could have eaten holes in any thickness of wood. The house began to burn.*

This was the "fire storm." Above the roar I ran to check Karon and the other side of the house. She was still putting out small fires with her "drinking fountain" water pressure. I looked down and saw the grass below the house, as if at the base of a cyclone, burning in a strong circular pattern. Though only short dry grass, the air was superheated and whipped by the high wind, it shot beneath the house. I only hoped it would not ignite. On my way to check the other side of the house, a gust of superheated air flew by us. I could feel its size: It was a 10 foot diameter sphere of "too intense" heat. Were it not past in a few seconds, it couldn't have been withstood. Our eyes were sore, we were too hot, and we couldn't breathe. It was at this point I felt that this very well may be "it", death. We may really find out what it's like to be burned to death. My blood pressure was near the explosion point. I found out later that Karon had felt this "heat of death," too, and thought she might die. I went into the house and Karon must have gotten into the lee of the house. I opened the door, stepped inside and inhaled the now fragrant cool air, which had been trapped inside the house. I thought I would check the upper deck around our main house and so ran to get the hose, brought it back, hauled it in through the door. Part of it hung up between the jamb and the door. I wrenched it free, ran up the circular stairs to the deck, hooked it into the hose bib and forced the water into the burning eave crevices. The fire went out - elation! I saw the other corner eave aflame. The hose would not reach. Ran back - shut off the water (save pressure) - ran half way around the deck - filled bucket (deathly slow) - ran back half around the deck to burning eave - doused with water (only half out) - ran back half around the deck - filled with water (interminable) - ran back half around the deck - doused with water (almost out) - ran half around the deck to hose bib - filled with water - ran a quarter way around the deck - heard Karon scream from inside - dropped bucket - opened sliding glass door, near panicked, ran three steps into the living room and was appalled to find myself in near-total darkness, enveloped in black, oily smoke - clearly different from the smoke of the brushfire outside.

I went deeper into the blackness and called, "Karon! Karon! Where are you?" I felt the top of the handrail of the circular stairway and cried louder. I was playing a part in a television serial. It wasn't real. I wasn't there. In my mind's eye I saw Karon lying in the children's bathroom, overcome and silent. (I couldn't breathe.) Or was she in the children's rooms? (I couldn't see.) If so, which room? (I couldn't stay much longer.) Or was she in the master bedroom or master bathroom. I called again. Then, faintly, through the noise and roar, the single welcome word, "Outside." I knew she had run down the circular stairway and out the front door to the motor court. She was safe; she had good, clean brushfire air to breathe. I ran to get air, too, on to the upper deck. Ran out of our once-beautiful house, now a glass mushroom brimful of poisonous black fumes.

The fires I'd left untended during the search were growing rapidly. The wind was still up. I ran to the opposite side of the house on the deck, leapt over the wooden handrail, swung down, hanging from the deck support and dropped five feet to the motor court below, ran to get Karon by the entry in the lee of the storm. The house was in flames. We ran in the only direction left - toward the driveway, past the pine trees and to the car. Our decisions were made. The game was up.

"Oh, Karon! Oh, honey!" The sudden realization of our loss dropped upon us then, except that our feelings couldn't accept the whole load. "Oh, Doug, our house." We tried to swallow what was happening to us but couldn't get it down. At the car now, "Doug, my purse? Inside the door." I looked toward the house, it's upper eaves burning, the motor court handrails beyond hope, the inside being consumed by God knows what kind of beast. And yet I did take three steps toward it, and then halted when a sheet of flame 15 feet high, 10 feet thick and 20 feet long hurtled across the driveway. The largest pine tree, the first in line, had exploded, flashed across my path, and ignited a similar pine tree on the other side of the drive, which also exploded.

Forget the purse! Door slams, tires screech, laying rubber up the hill through flames each side of the driveway to the roadway past our neighbors' burning houses and onto Malibu Canyon road. Our children! Our own children in the Malibu Civic Center lobby with Salvation Army punch and donuts and tears and streaky faces. Up the hill, our house was just getting "to it." Whimpers, tears, reassurances weakly rendered, coffee on an unwilling stomach.

To clinch it for me, I walked outside to take a last look. I leaned against the open Civic Center column for a long time. Over there, police and civilians watched 'er burn as I did. Seen through the smoke, the pretty house on the hill, blazing, flowing, roaring, licking into the clouds. An orange ball with black silhouettes I recognized as handrails and posts and decks and roof. What a blaze! What a house!

That night the Yellin's had fresh sheets, separate beds for our children. Our recovery had begun. Our dog, Daisy, was with us, too. Our three cats, Peek-a-boo, Poobah and Suki were lost. The quiet of the Yellin's home was a balm to shattered nerves.

In the days that followed, it was hard to experience the complete disaster. The memories, rather, would come up one at a time. Admiring a friend's music stand I said, "Hey, I have one just like it." Then I'd remember the loss of the children's pictures, the movies of Lili's first steps and all the birthday parties, a fine mural given me by Richard Haines, a close friend, a classic Hans Wegner sewing cabinet, Karon's much-used and much loved sewing machine, her hand-hooked rug, my mother's knitted sweaters, socks, things for the family. Fifty of my paintings in a suitcase, and all my working drawings for the past 15 years; the cats.

In the light of saving our lives, I don't at all mind the loss of our home. After all, we almost had three orphans. The air is still as sweet. The sights are still as good (except in Malibu Canyon), and our friends are friendlier than ever. I have my brain, my hands, my wife and family. I am overwhelmed with the generosity of everyone. In fact, it has opened up a marvelous new dimension of life I only suspected. Food, clothing, places to stay, offers of money. We'll always be amazed, heartened and grateful. After all, a house becomes a habit. House and family become fused. Eliminate the house and... We called our parents immediately to tell them the news. "Operator, I'd like to place a call to Mr. P. F. Rucker in Golden, Colorado. I want to charge it to my home phone."

37. Doug in Home section article shown after the fire. (Not a happy camper.) Dick Gross, photographer.

McMasters included a before picture of the house contrasting with the burned remains and the forlorn picture on the previous page.

YELLINS'

*S*till in shock that first night our family was invited to the house of friends and former clients, the Yellin's, in Santa Monica Canyon where we received caring, sympathy and great amounts of love. We arrived well after dusk and were thankful to be cleaned up and fed. Exhausted, we got out of our clothes that reeked of smoke and in a state of bewilderment and disbelief welcomed hot showers and borrowed pajamas. In a dazed existence we passed the night, each breath exhaling the strong smell of brush smoke that had saturated our lungs. Daisy our loving and gentle dog probably curled up on the covers at the foot of one of the children's beds.

38. Pedestal house after fire.

The fire was still raging the next day, but losing strength. Police and Fire Officials kept people out of the disaster area, but within a day or two we managed to get back to our site, the place where our house used to be.

39. Shocked Rucker family.

The sight of steel beams lying flat like spaghetti on gray ashes was devastating. Tangled conduit, bits of semi-recognizable crockery and molten glass in shapes like devilish sculptures added to our dismay. Where once was a beautiful structure, now there was nothing but ashes and debris. Our family couldn't comprehend the weight of this disaster. Thereafter, we would be forced to play life by the numbers. I had a family to support. We needed permanent living quarters, new clothes, food, toothbrushes, soap and combs. My face looked shady because my beard *(I use the term loosely because I don't have much of one.)* was growing and I needed a razor. I had to buy a wallet and order duplicates of my credit cards. I had to reinstate my driver's and architectural licenses and obtain copies of my birth certificate, social security number university degree and architectural license. Karon needed personal things too, as well as our young girls. We had fled fire fighting dressed in jeans and T-shirts and the children had whatever was on their backs; their school clothes. I had no place to work.

The Yellin's hospitality was soon relieved when our friends the Resnick's and their three children invited us to stay at their house for a week or so in the Serra Retreat. To understand for myself what had actually happened, it was there I wrote *Death of a House*. Our family still carries thanks in our hearts for the Resnik family's generosity.

Afterward, we were invited by Karon's divorced friend, Sandy Berman to stay for a short period in her apartment on the beach. A former dancer, Sandy was also artistic, poetic, cultured and educated. This refined person was also a single parent raising three children. Since she had only two bedrooms in her ocean-front apartment it was crowded, but with her loving attitude and her two older children finding another place to sleep, she helped us piece our lives together during our time of crisis. At this time, s*elfless*, would describe Sandy. She had also seen the darker side of life and was working through a portion of it herself. Sandy's young daughter, Laurie, slept with our youngest ones during those nights and insisted we take her bedroom while she slept on the living room couch. We appreciated Sandy and Laurie and love them to this day.

While we stayed with Sandy we were introduced to her fiancé, Hal Letven, an energetic, enthusiastic businessman and former flyer in World War II. Hal was originally from Chicago and had invented a system of paying blue-collar workmen through vouchers called Money Orders that could be redeemed from booths rather than from the bank. The *Money Order* business prospered and he and his partner were monetarily rewarded. Hal was to enter my life more significantly as a client later on.

40. Viveka at 10 years old observing disaster.

I remember Sandy and her daughter, Laurie, who was slightly younger than Viveka, and our family of five sitting on sofas around the living room coffee table listening to the crash of waves and the noisy sea past the short deck while we ate fried chicken and salad with rice. While there, Karon and I were overwhelmed with condolence letters from friends, former clients, relatives and strangers. Some included hard cash, fifty or a hundred dollars, and some were sympathetic responses to the *Death of a House* article I'd written.

Letters from Mary Batcheller of North Hollywood and Jan Duncan from Corona del Mar were two I saved that were particularly helpful. They understood our plight and sympathized. Other letters of sympathy and support came from different parts of the country, some as far as Steamboat Springs, Colorado, Chicago and Florida.

President Nixon declared Malibu a National Disaster Area. Articles about the fire sprung up in the Malibu Times and Surfside News and volunteer shops materialized to collect and distribute free clothing and incidentals to make life livable for the homeless once again. Our family found better clothing at volunteer shops than we'd had before the fire. Karon and I were astounded at the generosity of the Malibu community. My favorite was a raglan shouldered, black silk shirt made by Gucci.

41. Viv, not letting circumstances get her down.

One of the field deputies, a friend of Sandy Berman and Hal Letven was a person bent on helping those in need. He found and distributed to me a free drafting table, parallel, triangles, electric eraser, and other items necessary to rebuild my architectural practice. Joe McCloskey, proprietor of Malibu's only art store, offered me free office space in the building in which he was renting. It was the old Rindge Railroad Terminal Building, an ancient gabled structure sheathed in rusting corrugated metal that later became a hardware store and then offices and stores. The room I was to occupy had a broad wall with minimal windows that looked across Pacific Coast Highway to the ocean. My entrance off the rear alleyway was shared with an antique warehouse and a dance studio. My new office had formerly been a pottery studio and the five-hundred-square-feet of floor was thickly covered with splattered clay. It wasn't pretty and the room had negligible light. Conversion to the clean operation of an architect's studio would require work, but it was *free* and artist-boss, Joe McCloskey, renewed my hope. Motivated by forty-two-year-old-career-building-energy, I'd swiftly return to work and was raring to go!

(Digression: May K. Rindge's old corrugated iron building had historical significance. It used to be her personal railroad terminal built to load and unload cattle waiting to be shipped to market on her own privately owned railroad. When cattle days were over, it became a hardware store run by a local contractor named Herve Babineau and then metamorphosed into a group of shops.)

42. Historic Rindge Terminal Building - Exterior view from Malibu Pier (My window - 5th from right side bldg.)

43. Alley entrance to Dance and Architectural Studios.

44. Replacement of new building circa 2000 on former Rindge property.

MRS. MUDD

After our two-week stay with Sandy, Mrs. Mudd offered us an apartment over her garage in the Malibu Movie Colony. We accepted and were in great appreciation for her kind and altruistic frame of mind.

Letter – No Date
Dear Mother and Dad,

...Also, I have almost sure prospects on three clients who want to rebuild after the fire. There were over forty houses totally destroyed in the relatively affluent Malibu Canyon area. One house should run about $80,000.00. One about $60,000.00. One about $35,000.00. ...The Pedestal House in some respects was our job, but financially it was also killing us. Now that it's gone, it's a funny kind of relief.

People have been super-generous to us since the fire. The girl next door in the Colony who must be younger than Karon, has five kids and has offered us unlimited use of her washer-dryer, has organized a work crew, and has already cleaned the entire apartment, washed all the windows, changed the curtains, brought over bed linens, and carpeted the place - just out of the goodness of her of her heart. It's fantastic!

Councilman Bradley's field deputy, Masomori Kojima, a boyhood friend of Karon's girlfriend, Sandy Berman, has political connections with large architectural firms in Los Angeles and promises I will have my electric typewriter, calculator, blueprint machine and all the equipment I'll need for a new office. He has also organized a clean up crew for this Saturday to clean our site. Also, I have a large workspace donated to me by Joe McCloskey who manages the local art and bookstore. It's a great spot and location. I have and we all have a better wardrobe than that with which we started.

Things are looking good. We plan to rebuild and will qualify for a 3% disaster loan. I will build a smaller, fireproof house this time. We have had offers of a loan from eight or so friends of up to $12,000.00, which we will not take if we don't have to.

We have $1,200.00 worth of gifts that were impossible to refuse, so all of this to say, we are doing fine and are in an up frame of mind. You don't have to worry about us we are

better than ever.
Sincerely, Doug.

LINC'S LETTER

Karon and I were pleased when an important old college friend responded to our loss. Linc Jones was a roommate of mine in the 1949 fall semester at the University of Illinois. A friend and dedicated student, he was a few years older than me but had arrived in the architecture department two years behind me. In 1950 after I graduated I stood up for him in his wedding party. He was a handsome young man, slim at five feet ten with dark brown hair and had graduated from Wright Junior College in Chicago before he came to Illinois. An excellent swimmer, he had been on Wright's rowing team. At Illinois he was dead serious about his chosen profession and I envied the ease with which he seemed to move through life.

After graduating high in his class he moved to Denver with his small family to open his own architectural office and did incredibly well there designing homes, apartments, and one Civic Center that showed great love for his hero, Frank Lloyd Wright, including Wright's *"integral ornament."* His letter:

Letter - January 19, 1971
Dear Doug, Karon, Vivi, Mandy, and Lilianne,
A friend of mine just sent me an article from the Los Angeles Times entitled, "Death of a House". I was completely shocked and disbelieving. Words seem so meaningless after hearing of your tragedy; but, as your friend, I know how desperately you and Karon must have fought to save your home. Your story, though tragic, was so well written that you should be an author, too.

I am thankful that you and your family are well, and that somehow you have bounced back. ...I don't know how it's possible. You always did have a strong philosophy about life and values, and I envy you in that regard. It sounds like your friends have all pitched in to help your family in the interim, which is gratifying.

I immediately called your brother's house and talked to Ellen, who brought me up to date on the aftermath, and also gave me your address.

I am happy that people have been so good to your family in every way.

I want to do something, mainly to make you laugh; so I am sending a 1908 Sears catalog with a $1,779.00 house, complete with plans, etc. This is one of my favorite volumes in my library. Money is meaningless at this point, but I want you to use the enclosed check ($200) to replenish your library, or for whatever purpose you feel is most useful.

Please accept my heartfelt condolences on your incomprehensible misfortune. Always feel that you and your family are welcome in our home, and you are always welcome to be a part of my architectural firm. I know that you and Karon have the strength to regroup and forge ahead. Your article was very moving and sounded just like you.

Please call or write when you can.
Your friend, Linc

Reply - January 22, 1971
Dear Lincoln,
Your crazy catalog, letter and gift-check came in the mail today. I was overwhelmed. Your generosity is too much. It was a great thing you did and I appreciate it more than I can express. Your check will really come in handy since I was not insured except for the amount of the mortgage. Our personal effects were estimated at about $35,000.00 and our equity at not less than $50,000 so you can see we dropped quite a lot. We came out of it with our kids, dog, selves, shoes, and

levis and that's all. In spite of this we are doing fantastically well these days. We have had friends come to the rescue time after time, donating time clothing, furniture, and some money, even artwork. Some even seemed to take it upon themselves to single handedly raise the Rucker family up on its feet. We are standing now thanks to friends I didn't know we had. You really find out who they are, by the way, which is always interesting.

Right after the fire a lady (Mrs. Mudd) who had an apartment over her garage in the Malibu Colony on the beach offered it to us. We stayed there for about two months while I tried to rebuild some kind of office. An owner of an art store friend of mine had some space at the back of his store and offered it to me rent-free until I could get back on my feet. Friends of mine came in and helped me construct tables, bookshelves, light-troughs, indoor trellis, etc. to get the office going. Then other victims of the fire, some that I knew and some that I didn't, came in to see me to talk about rebuilding. I was happy about that, sent for contracts to the A. I. A. (American Institute of Architects) and took retainers and before I knew it here I am in business again in a new location. I have about five house jobs and one restaurant addition to do. I just put on my second man and seem to be very quickly pulling out of the hole. I've got about $3,500.00 more to go, though, to the I. R. S. for "69" Federal Taxes. That's a long story that I'll go in to sometime if you're interested on your next trip to California to see us. In the meantime the Federal Government, who had declared Malibu a national disaster situation, is renting us a place in a large condominium here in Malibu. They will pick up the tab until September '71 at which time we will once more have to be self-sufficient.

Rest assured, the Rucker family is doing well for now. See you, Doug

FIRE PICTURES

Our family made progress despite disturbing photos that took time in presenting themselves. While alone painting the floor in my new studio, the thought of the house burning down struck me funny. I laughed with tears at the irony. After all I'd been through, dragging my family in search of a dream, Gordon dying of cancer, long-suffering about bills, and the fact that Karon and the children had been happier in Santa Monica Canyon and that our new house had literally gone up in smoke. I'd yanked our family out of their happy nest to accompany me on a wild goose chase. If Gordon hadn't met his untimely death, perhaps we'd have sold the house and things might have been different. But freeing myself to do something different, getting a second trust deed from Gus with low interest and no payments for three years, Gordon's death, our severe financial struggles, and then when I can see daylight and am about to *win*, the house burns down with all our personal affects, our classic furniture, artwork and every material thing. Look not elsewhere, the joke's on us!

45. Easter card to Grandpa and Grandma. Love, Lilianne.

46. House before the fire.

47. House about to be engulfed.

48. House engulfed.

49. Remains as seen from the west.

50. Remains from above.

A Tale of Two Houses

Architect Fred Lyman who had received significant publishing in the Los Angeles Times lost his prize-winning oriental house too. It had been built as a fire-resistant structure, but Fred and I who were the *new kids on the block* and showing everyone how to live the *"good"* life, allowed our houses to be burned to the ground. Architect's who should have known better constructed *"straw houses"* instead of *"brick"* houses. We build homes of wood, exposed underneath and surrounded by heavy brush, and ready like tinder to be ignited for a glorious bonfire. How embarrassing! How ridiculous! How absurd! If we were in architectural class, we should have been given an *"F"* for practicality.

In the next house I'd do the most important deterrent, *build with stucco exterior, close off the bottom of the house, and maintain brush clearance.*

MAISON DE VILLE

Since Malibu had been declared a National Disaster Area, the California Fair Plan Insurance Company was allowed to grant us a free lease of an apartment for one year, at which time our family was expected to have made a full recovery. Therefore, on or about February first, 1971, we moved into a Maison De Ville condominium.

51. Maison De Ville from Pacific Coast Highway.

When I was doing consultation work for the Adamson Companies I had reviewed plans for this very same condominium. I had thought the plans well detailed and despite a bias for my own particular style deemed the Maison De Ville well-thought-out and harmoniously designed.

52. Maison De Ville pool

We were grateful the U. S. Government was going to pay burned-out family's rent through September. Karon and I as strong members of our small chorus continued our weekly singing and every couple of months participated in a concert. Karon's soloist voice with substantial vibrato was almost too strong for Renaissance chorus work. Though a voice should be strong, it shouldn't overwhelm others in the section. Better musicians know pitch, come in on time, and stay on tempo. They love the music, diminish with pianissimo, and swell with crescendos. I was strong on *love-the-music,* but amateurish at pitch, timing, tempo and the rest of it. I'm fond of saying, *"I'm best at crescendos."*

Our condominium two-story apartment had the kitchen, dining, and living room downstairs with a sizeable deck overlooking the highway and ocean. Upstairs was the master bedroom and bath with a children's bedroom with bath off the hall. Two would sleep in a bunk bed and one separate.

53. *A very tired family. Lilianne, Amanda, Karon, Doug and Viveka at the Maison De Ville condominium.*

There were forty-eight units in the complex, each 1,600 square feet around a sunny, sixty-foot pool. Landscaping, driveways and parking next to the building surrounded the pool and bathhouse. On the north was a long tile-roofed carport of a post and beam nature supported on ten-inch diameter pilings driven in the earth. Inhabitants thought children would inhibit their activities and devalue units and so original regulations prohibited them, though by 1970 this was unconstitutional. In a National Disaster the government could provide burned out families a place to live. Were existing owners to challenge the U. S. Government, they feared they'd make an issue of their original restrictions resulting in possible loss of their apartment.

Most neighbors were pleasant, but that doesn't mean *all* were pleasant. There were a few glowering faces, particularly from those dozing with a paper or magazine on chaise lounges while the children were in the pool. Karon and I warned the children not to make noise and though we may be biased, I found them cooperative. There were no official complaints during our stay.

We were comforted when Bill and Ann Duke and their two children, Billy and Kathleen, moved into a downstairs apartment. Bill Duke worked for Litton Industries in the Advanced Marine Technology Division and was responsible for design of the entire electronics system for a single ship. Anne had just finished grad school at Irvine University and was working at Rockwell International Science Center developing research software. The Dukes home had also been burned and the Duke family became our close and lasting friends. Viveka and Kathleen are friends to this day.

EVENING OUTLOOK ARTICLE

On November 4th Karon and I were in The Topanga Festival of Olden Music. An article in the Evening Outlook follows:

Malibu Architect Doug Rucker, and his wife Karon lost their showplace Malibu Canyon home and all their possessions in the September fire. Among their possessions were costumes they wore while performing with the Neo Renaissance Singers. Despite the travail of relocating home and business after the fire, the Rucker's found time to rehearse and to make new costumes for the upcoming Topanga Festival of Olden Music. According to John Leicester, president of the Neo-Renaissance, the devotion of the Rucker's is typical of the approximately 16 members. Most are professional people, including doctors and lawyers drawn together by

54. Photo in Evening Outlook, November 4, 1970

their love of 15th and 16th century music, Leicester said. They come from all over the county, as far away as Carson, to rehearse at Leicester's Pacific Palisades home.

Proceeds of the festival go to the Topanga Community House and to the non-profit Foundation of the Neo-Renaissance. Among events at which the group performs is the Pleasure Faire held in Agoura.

Letter excerpt – November 23, 1970
Dear Mother and Dad,
…Enclosed is an article on the fire. I finely got a "by" line. It's fun to write. I'd really like to do more if only I had the time. Exxie Lee Battle, our former cleaning woman, when she'd hear me complain of not having enough time, would say, "My goodness! All the good Lord give us is time. We have nothing but time. That's all."

And really she is right. All we do have is time. We have to be choosy on how to spend it. We are still getting settled at the Maison De Ville. You may remember that large building westerly from the house. It looked like a group of apartments, but is really a condominium. Our plans are to build again on the same site, but you might say we are going to take our time with it and not just rush into it. I have a lot of work to do right now which is one good thing that has come out of the fire. I'm building back three or four burnouts. The clients I have are reputable types. I have a draftsman, even. His name is Lew Dominy, a Southern California University Traveling Scholarship winner with one-year experience. He is an eager guy, and I think I'll enjoy working with him. He's been with me a week and seems to like his job.

Our Topanga singing concert went well. Thirteen of us sang works by Heinrich Isaac. A mass. The Missa Carmingum. It's a beautiful work and was enjoyable to sing. I even was part of a bass quartet, my first experience with that sort of thing.

Karon and the kids are fine. They seem to be adjusting

A Tale of Two Houses

to all the changes as well as to be expected. I think things will settle down a little if we can just stay in one place for a reasonable period of time. The changes of location are a little trying.

Must run to mail this. Hope you are all right. We got your last letter and really enjoyed it.
Love, Doug

SCANNING MALIBU

On December 3, 1970, Dorothy Stotsenberg, writer for the Santa Monica Evening Outlook, in one of her weekly articles said:

Did you know - Malibu architect, Doug Rucker, designed the beautiful clubhouse for the Point Dume Club? This spacious Spanish-style building truly shows Doug's versatility - it's quite a change from his usual wood-steel-glass houses.

55. Dorothy Stotsenberg

Of course I loved being mentioned in her article and appreciated the complement, but if you look closely at the Point Dume Club design, you'll see the same old post-and-beam is still working.

Ed Stotsenberg, Dorothy Stotsenberg's husband, holds the world running championship for the 500 and 1,000 meters in the fifty-plus age group. Both have passed on after living in their forward thinking Frank Lloyd Wright style contemporary home they built for themselves high in the Malibu hills off Mulholland Drive. I presume they have given donations to many institutions, but I know and admire them for their contribution to students of Pepperdine with a gift of the Stotsenberg Track. For these gifts and offers of money, Karon and I were extremely grateful. They made us feel accompanied in our plight and that encouraged us to recuperate.

56. Doug at new office entrance.

NEW OFFICE

It was essential I get a new office up and running. Joe McCloskey allowed me to use the empty studio formerly rented by clay-sculpture artist, John Schulps. It was a mess! Walls and floor were covered with thick clay. A low wall of exposed two-by-fours with plywood on the back separated the empty space from the adjacent dance studio. Ceilings were high and made of thin boards over purlins and trusses roofed with corrugated metal, the overhead wood ridden with termites whose droppings like poppy-seeds rained unceasingly.

57. Architectural studio after several years in operation.

I worked evenings and weekends removing clay from the walls and scraping the floor, then washing it on hands and knees. When dry I finished it with a several coats of greenish Olympic wood stain that contrasted with redwood bender board I'd attached to an existing wall of open studs. A carpenter friend, Fritz Schafer, made a support from new four-by-fours for another gift; a large, heavy, flat filing cabinet for working drawings. Flat files were from an unknown but compassionate architect and delivered through the generosity of deputy to Supervisor, Burton Chase, Masimori Kojima.

A fiber-artist friend of Karon needed a storage place for her work. It had been part of a large outdoor art experience at the Santa Monica Pier beach and included several other pieces of similar size that viewers were to walk through. I thought it attractive when draped around the office. Karon included her own fiber hanger for a pot of plants over my conference desk.

58. Architectural studio looking north toward entry on left.

Deputy Masimori Kojima, came up with a classic three –foot-by-four-foot-six inch wood drafting table for use at home. He also supplied another indestructible metal-framed drafting table that would last a lifetime. I kept this for personal use in the new office. Three new hollow core doors were supported off the wall by slim diagonal wood braces and would be used by draftsmen. Stools I purchased from Heibert's Furniture Company. They were well-constructed and built for library use. Daughter Viveka and I yet have three still in good condition. Harry Heckendorf made a conference table out of a three-foot by six-foot cabinet top salvaged from one of his remodeling jobs. It had an interesting shiny-black Formica top trimmed in natural oak. Friend-photographer Richard Gross donated blow-ups of the Knebel house glued to masonite and suitable for hanging. He used old negatives taken for the Home section article in 1968.

59. Doug on telephone in new office.
Knebel house pictures in background.

Fritz, my carpenter friend, installed an indoor trellis of two-by-tens that I painted Oxford Brown, enlarged a window, hung a used glass door with colored panels from one of my former remodeling jobs and repaired a section of wall for the installation of four-inch wide by one-fourth-inch horizontal redwood bender boards I installed myself. He also built a platform to support a plywood top holding tubes of finished plans and my new Dart blue-line printer. A couple of filing cabinets completed the room.

60. Respected friends and draftsmen, Richard Sol, Toby Watson and Doug signing OK! (Background - new entry.)

At the same time I was moving into the new office, a commercial building housing one of my attorney clients was being torn down. I had designed a unique exterior entry for my former attorney client consisting of a short side screen and minimal trellis. On this he had lettered, *(His name) Attorney,* but letters had been removed. Hardly more than a year old, I hated to see his entry demolished with the whole building. So one Sunday Fritz and I took his truck with hammers, pliers, nail-pullers, and other equipment to the intersection of Webb Way and Pacific Coast Highway near Malibu Road and in broad daylight audaciously removed the entire entrance piece, loaded it into the truck and drove away.

61. *Melaleuca among the planter boxes and Lilianne.*

Disassembled in half, it was lying at an ungainly angle bridging the back of his truck, while we headed for the backside of the Rindge Terminal Building. The following day, instead of *(His name) Attorney* it was installed as *DOUG RUCKER, Architect.* I then built a couple of planters from redwood boards around the existing concrete slab, planted it with ground cover and a Melaleuca, and *VOILA!* an entry.

FAMILY LIFE

Through the generosity of Mrs. Mudd, our family stayed almost two months over her garage in the Malibu Movie Colony before moving into the Maison De Ville where we continued as circumstances would allow, to live normally.

I drove Viveka and her friend, Laurie Berman, to springboard diving lessons at the Santa Monica City College pool on Wednesdays and Fridays.

Though Lilianne had no lessons for two or three months, she resumed piano lessons she'd begun a year ago. For six years, Lili's interest never flagged and I was and am always proud of her enthusiasm and passion for good music.

Amanda continued to sketch on everything available, humming and singing while she worked, and on occasions I complemented her sketches and told her, *"You sound good, Mandy."*

Karon continued teaching arts and crafts to children at Webster Elementary and once a week we hired a sitter and traveled to Pacific Palisades for singing rehearsal.

For my birthday, mother sent me a gift certificate to a bookstore, *(Barnes and Noble)* and I bought and read *The Immense Journey* and *The Unexpected Universe*, both by Lauren Eisley. The *Immense Journey* influenced me greatly and I began to understand geologic time and its necessity to develop even the tiniest living creature. I was astounded that nature, apparently starting from nothing, could develop an organ so complex as the *eye.* To think that a living creature could detect colors and perspective by eyes placed inches apart that was communicated to the brain and upon that information could decide on how to act was beyond belief. I was thunderstruck by the idea and miracle of life. Though I'd known it all intellectually, Eisley explained it so I could *hear* and understand it. I discussed ideas in *The Immense Journey* with my eldest, Viveka. She was fascinated and though only eleven understood the complexities as well. In fact, Viv seemed the only person in my family that *could* grasp these overwhelmingly archetypal concepts.

For our birthday's, *(Doug's of December 31st, Karon's on January 4th,)* we gave each other our customary gift, a subscription to the Los Angeles County Art Museum. We attended a performance later, featuring the New York Pro-Musica Organization singing the best of Renaissance Music.

Letter excerpt - *February 28, 1971*
Dear Mother and Dad,
It's Sunday and I have decided to relax today. Karon has been reading a book all day and is quiet. Vivi is recovering from a bout with the flu and is reading the Sunday funnies. Lili is quiet doing I don't know what. Mandy, I think, is watching TV. Anyway, at this moment (and probably only for a moment) things are calm and relaxed. I have had a busy week, but now I lie on the top floor of our condominium home in our mussed up bed and listen to the traffic on Pacific Coast Highway. It is 3:00 PM in the afternoon and the sun, though out and bright, is slanting steeply through the floor-to-ceiling sliding glass bedroom door. I look out through the handrail balcony railing and see a big stretch of the ocean; almost all ocean and sky outside our bedroom door/window. Today we got our westerly wind back after four days of buffeting by the Santana (southeasterly) winds. It's good to have our westerly back. It means that all is well, things are back to normal and we can relax. I never know

what a Santana might blow up. It whipped the fire through here last September.

Guess what? Everything was so relaxed (like in a Sunday hammock with just a fly buzzing somewhere) that I put down my pen and paper and just took an hour and a half nap. Wow! Did that feel good!

And now David Riehl, our oldest living friend, will be coming over at 6:00 PM. It is now 5:00 PM and any moment now Karon will fly at me to clean up or prepare for something. So with fear that this note to you may go unfinished, I will list the news:

(1) Office: I am busier than ever. Clients seem to be coming in droves. I have two wonderful draftsmen and we are getting work out as best we can. All jobs are interesting. Money is coming in and as of this weekend I believe I will be caught up with all my bills. That has got to be some kind of record since I haven't been able to say that for many a year.

(2) Karon is still teaching crafts and though our…
(Yes! I was just interrupted…)

It is now 9:00 PM. David Riehl is here. We have eaten dinner and he is looking through the want ads. He's unemployed at the moment as are a lot of people in Southern California. The children are in bed. I have just finished reading them another chapter of J. R. Tolkien's, The Hobbit, which they and I find fascinating. I enjoy the reading part, too, and can understand what joy actors must get allowing beautiful words to trip off their tongues.

(3) Vivi has the flu with a temperature of 101 to 103. We keep it down with aspirin and I'm sure she'll be fine, but she's been down for four days and is bored and anxious to go to school. She still takes diving lessons, has just begun guitar lessons, and has been taking sewing lessons. Karon has just started her knitting a scarf. She's doing quite well.

(4) Lili still takes her piano and is a joy to be near. She's such a sensitive child. Loved by teachers and students alike.

(5) Mandy, our super-girl is also a joy to have around

except a bit overwhelming at times. She is taller and heavier than Lili who will be nine on April 8th. She is having more trouble reading than the other two did and personal interaction may be a future strong point with her rather than studiousness.

(6) Karon was presented with an award for Outstanding Service to the school. (Webster Elementary) She is a teachers aid and teaches after-school crafts and helps in many ways. The award was presented by the P. T. A. and consisted of a lifetime membership pin. It was given at the monthly meeting night and I was called up to pin it on her. I was quite proud. She certainly was deserving.

(7) We at the office have been so busy working on other jobs that Karon and I have given virtually no thought to our own home. We have several thoughts on the matter, but I would rather tell you about it than try to write it.

Enough news! We would like to invite you to Southern California to visit us. We can fix you up somewhere here. I probably won't be able to take too much time off, but Saturday and Sunday would be OK and I can manage evenings. It would still be worthwhile. Hope you are well and happy. We miss you.
Much love, Doug

62. Viveka, Lilianne, Amanda.
In background - Surfrider Beach.

63. Phil and Eva Rucker

PARENT'S VISIT

Mother and dad decided to visit us by driving from Golden Colorado to Sunny Southern California. Having driven the distance myself I suspect they drove along dangerous precipices and were awed by dazzling views while descending breathtaking slopes for thousands of feet. I'm sure they went through wide, grassy valleys to come unexpectedly upon intimate villages tucked among the dark green of healthy trees alongside a winding river and that the villages seemed a wonderful place to live. Then through wind-driven desert with heavy clouds in the distance, black at the bottom, laden with electricity and lightning driving unpredictable bolts like hammers into the ground. Then the busy freeways and smog of L. A.

"How was your trip, dad?"
"We made good time."

64. Vivi, Mandy, Karon, Lili.

FEELINGS ABOUT THE YEAR

Our former house burned on September 25, 1970. Vivi's 11th birthday was on September 12, 1971. Almost a year had passed since the fire and you'd think I'd have some feelings for the year. I was sorry about the catastrophe. To lose our dream house after only four years of occupancy was bad for an architect, but afterward I was deluged with enough work to drown me. Fortunately, as a young man of forty-two with a wife, three daughters and a dog, I evidently had enough energy. I didn't give our unpleasant experience much thought because I had too much office work to do; people to hire, clients to meet. At home I had kids to keep occupied, an artistic wife with interests in weaving and singing, chorus practice two nights a week, running a couple of miles a day, children's lessons to drive to, etc. Our lives were so hectic, it's surprising I had time for any thoughts or feelings at all.

As to Karon's feelings, since there was no other way to deal with a life-blow like losing a treasured home with its hard-earned furniture and personal items such as still pictures of your kids early life, Karon rose to the challenge and worked hard at what needed doing. I assumed her feelings or lack of feelings were the same as mine and we were unable to do more than that which lay directly before us. From Karon's standpoint that meant teaching after school arts and crafts, pursuing weaving, taking singing lessons and participating in chorus work.

As to the feelings of my children, that's for them to say. As I saw them, they were apparently OK; going to school, making friends, going to lessons, doing homework, and involved in children's day-to-day activities. They looked OK and me, having nothing to compare our situation to, assumed they were OK. Sometimes assumptions can be deceiving and it was possible that the new circumstances were affecting all our lives and working their spells on our unconscious minds. The fire experience and aftermath was having its affect and I suspect none of us knew what that affect was. Though I've lived a positive life, there were times when it seemed we were found *by* bad luck - or we *found* bad luck. Hence, a notice from the I. R. S.

A Tale of Two Houses

THE I. R. S.

We were notified by mail and then visited by an Internal Revenue Service man dressed in casual business clothes. We were surprised and appalled to discover we were being audited. I later learned the I. R. S. frequently audits those people who have had a sudden loss. After discretely letting our dilemma be known to certain friends, we found a sympathetic and experienced young married man named Bill Hoppe who courageously took it upon himself to help. I don't know whether we found Bill or Bill found us. It's a mystery, but I appreciated Bill then and appreciate him now. He encouraged us to give in when necessary, but minimize our debt when justified.

After reading the instructions he said we'd have to compile a list of everything we owned with an estimate of it's value to the I. R. S. Compiling such a list is brain draining and time consuming. It taxed our limited time and memories. Hair hung down over my sweaty brow as I detailed and calculated the endless items. Karon was disturbed and cranky. The list was long. I became aware of the many things we'd acquired and guessed at their value.

Presenting our work sheets to Bill, he put it together in an organized form and acted as our representative and buffer to the United States Government. The examiner took the information with him and we didn't hear from him for about two weeks at which time he mailed us a return that showed we owed the government $3,000.00 for our 1970 taxes. The examiner never explained his calculations, but in looking over the tax form it was obvious he was convinced the figures shown were not true and that we were practicing tax evasion.

Upon facing him and objecting about the amount and telling him we had lost our home, our business, and all our possessions with no insurance other than for our mortgage, and we had to begin over again with home, school, work, and that we were pressed for money, he claimed no one with a family of five could have survived on as small an income as we'd shown. Therefore, it was incumbent upon him to charge us $3,000.00, the amount he apparently calculated based on what we *should* have earned for minimum survival.

LIFE SAVERS

Early in January I found myself with *about* five jobs. The first was a large house for the Myerly's in the Serra Retreat. I signed the contract and did preliminary drawings, but I used the word *about* in the sentence above because at the time of the letter the Myerly house *seemed* like a real job. In February, due to personal reasons, the Myerly's quit. So I really had four jobs - still too much for one person.

The first *real* job was for Kathie Blake, a divorced lady with four teenagers whose rickety old house on an ocean bluff off Malibu Road had burned to ashes that blew to the sea. The second was for a middle-aged bachelor named Schiff who'd owned a house in Malibu's Roberts Ranch on a sloping bluff, west and high above Coral Canyon. The third was for Jack and Terri Ford, another couple who'd lost their Malibu Road beach house and the fourth for Mr. and Mrs. Halpin, again, victims of the fire.

LEW DOMINY

Busy enough to be in a panic, I let word out to other architect's and called USC for promising students. My efforts produced immediate results. Lew Dominy walked in the door. A tall, athletic young man with thin, dark hair prematurely balding, who wore horn-rimmed glasses, he spoke quietly and seemed to know exactly what he wanted. *(To work under the personal attention of an architect within a small office to get a more intimate view of a bona fide architectural practice.)* In our interview I discovered he'd won a traveling scholarship to Europe from the University of Southern California, one of the best architectural schools in the United States.

65. Lew Dominy, Doug, Steve Wooley in alley outside office.

Just before graduation he'd lived in England, France, and Italy and had studied and sketched for three months before returning to get his Master's Degree. He was married with no children and a devout Protestant who coached a basketball team for the underprivileged at the church gym on weeknights and weekends. Like God's Great Gift, Lew spent Thanksgiving and Christmas bringing food and presents to the poor. In school he'd been a maker of superior architectural models and according to his friend, Steve Wooley, made his models so strong students could stand on them. This might have been a rumor, but I watched Steve's face and I don't think he was pulling my leg.

STEVE WOOLEY

Eventually, there was so much work I needed another man. Without hesitation, Lew recommended his closest friend, schoolmate and church member, Steve Wooley. I called him in for an interview and found him also to be a tall, dark and good looking young man, single and shy. As I came to know him he didn't appear to date much and seemed every bit as pious as Lew. Masculine by nature, his value system didn't seem at the moment to include girls. He talked slowly behind dark-rimmed glasses with reserved intelligence and I found him to be diligent and caring in his work. An easy person with whom to work, I came to like Steve and remember his smile and willingness to produce what we both thought was right.

RICHARD SOL

When Richard Sol was seventeen, long before he worked in my office, he was hitchhiking along Malibu Road when I picked him up in my Volvo. He later told me, *"The black Volvo looked like a London taxicab."* He'd studied piano and music at Santa Monica City College with a lovely lady, a piano teacher who'd once given a command performance for Franklin D. Roosevelt. After working with her for a semester she gently informed him he'd begun piano too late and warned him of the work and dedication involved to become a concert pianist. For Richard, the effort might have been OK, but when she questioned his ear for music, Richard became discouraged. He decided to finish the semester and then enter UCLA where he took two years of general courses majoring in Pre-Med making the honor roll in his third year. Dissatisfied with Pre-Med and following his heart, he entered the Architecture School at USC and asked me if I'd take him on as a junior draftsman during the summer between semesters.

I said, *"With no experience, you'll inhibit production."* He agreed to work *free*. I *heard* him at that point and decided he might be helpful to Lew and Steve doing menial work, printing, tracing, lettering, and clean-up. On his off hours and at home he might study plans and learn the somewhat standard practices of a small office. I liked Richard and ultimately he became a successful Malibu architect. He is happily married with three wonderful children in illustrious schools and remains a noble friend.

TOBY WATSON

After spending a brilliant year doing working drawings and making models, Lew declined my offer to share my architectural business and decided to move on. Enter Toby Watson, a tall, well-mannered young man with long, uncut brown hair and a mustache. Also a graduate from Southern California University, I immediately started him with a new job. Toby stayed with me for several years, eventually starting his own architectural practice in Venice, California. His artist wife, D. J. Hall, was an expert in colored pencils and oils.

66. Mustached Toby Watson, Richard Sol and Doug.

Letter excerpt - February 14, 1971
Dear Mother and Dad,
 ... Just had Henry and Lois Gibson in a few minutes ago. I will be doing preliminary studies on a master bedroom they plan on adding to the Dorr house they just bought. Henry is a wonderful, sweet guy, an ecologist nut and likable. He is something like a leprechaun. He has invited us (our family) to the Laugh-In special they are doing on the 21st of this month. He says we will see Arty Johnson at that time. (Arty, also a regular on Laugh-In, was former President of the Austin High School Student Government in June of 1945 when at the same time I was Austin's Senior Class President.) We'll see if it comes about. ... Everything's fine here. House to start construction in about a month. (I think!)
Doug

WHY OK TO BUILD

 (1) We owned two thirds of an acre with a positive

geology report overlooking Surfrider Beach in the heart of Malibu.

(2) Our driveway was paved to the site of a new house.

(3) We had a workable sewage disposal system.

(4) Our foundation system was usable sitting on twelve feet deep caissons tied together at the top with reinforced grade beams.

(5) Gas, water and electricity were stubbed to a new house begging for operation.

(6) Our grant deed even included the right to use a private beach on Malibu Road.

Our assets were many. *Radical change? Buy a new Malibu house?* What were we thinking? Perhaps building on a site with the most important problems already solved would be easier. As we pursued this kind of thinking, the more it took hold and soon I was designing a new house over the old foundations, getting excited and discussing it with Karon.

The pedestal house showed youthful enthusiasm. It was a work of the *heart*, but in no way was it a work of *head*. From a rational standpoint, the idea had been a cone of twigs built over flammable paper waiting for a match. When I thought of the new house I found myself saying, *"I don't want it to burn down twice in front of everybody!"* If the second house burned, comments would be, *"Won't that architect ever learn?"* I told Karon, *"If we build again it will be fireproof!"*

Karon corrected me, *"You mean fire-resistant?"*

"All right then, fire-resistant, but almost fireproof."

Letter excerpt - July 27, 1971
Dear Mother and Dad,
...I hope to submit plans for our new house to the Building Department this week. Our loan is for $50,000.00 and as usual I have designed something over the budget. Karon and I have fought and struggled over the design and now we each feel we have a house in which we can live. We

spent weeks hunting for new locations to live. We looked at lots of houses to buy, but could not come up with one we could identify with and afford. We decided to rebuild on our own footings and live with it.

I am taking springboard diving lessons with Vivi again after an eight-month layoff. I'm not too good, but enjoy the physical activity. I run about 1-1/2 miles or so every day in addition to diving and for several months was swimming 100 laps - one mile in the pool every day. I'm in pretty fair shape and weigh 161 to 164 pounds. I would like to get down to 154 to get that last spec of rubber-tire fat off my waist line. I have cut off all coffee and wine for over two years now. Once every three months I might have a beer and afterward I'm almost always sorry.   Love, Doug

RESNICKS

Our time limit for free rent as paid for by the U.S. Government ran out in September of 1971, therefore, something drastic was to happen regarding our living arrangements. We'd have to buy our condominium with $10,000.00 as a down payment committing ourselves to monthly mortgage payments, or else there was no other thinkable solution. Though business was improving rapidly, our extra savings were zero. Fortunately, Bernie and Rheta Resnick, out of the goodness of their hearts with the assumption we were worth it, lent us the down payment. We breathed a soulful sigh of relief and with a loan from Bernie and Rheta, purchased our apartment until we could sell it and move into our new house.

THE DESIGN

Though Karon and I and the children had lived in the now-burned pedestal house as if it were *our* house, it really had been *my* house. The actuality was that I had forced my family to live in *my* house. I designed the original pedestal house for speculation with encouragement from my soon to be deceased partner Gordon Ewert. The idea of Doug's and Gordon's *"spec"* house was only *mildly* interesting to Karon. She knew she would never live in it. It was Gordon's and my project and her input was non-existent. *"Yes, dear. That's good, dear."* In normal situations, since the husband is at work, a new house is really the *wife's* new house. That's where she occupies her time and she needs a house that fits her needs. She must feel comfortable in a house that's responsive to her daily work in raising children and providing a happy environment for the family as well as wanting it to be clean and comfortable for she and her husband when he comes home. For someone as creative as Karon not to have a say in her own house is almost sacrilegious. Having 0% input on the pedestal house she couldn't possibly think of it as hers. This time I wanted to incorporate *her* ideas and treat her as any other architect would - like a new client,

So I'd design a house and Karon would find something wrong with it. Sometimes I thought it was difficult for her to understand a prime rule of architecture, *two physical objects cannot occupy the same place at the same time.* I designed. She criticized. I designed and it was still not perfect. I must have tried a dozen schemes and we must have run into as many stalemates and she and I were both exasperated. I looked inwardly. Perhaps it was as we might both have suspected, I was limited by my talent.

I took to visualizing myself throwing all the design elements up in the air, kitchen, baths, living room, bedrooms, laundry room, entry, etc., like so many straws in the wind, hoping most would fall to the ground in recognizable piles showing a final basic consistency. Eventually, I had success. *(I sometimes use this imaginary technique on new clients today.)*

COMING TO TERMS

We were parents with three small children and a dog on a steeply sloping site with existing footings, limited parking, southeastern orientation and westerly winds. What were we going to do with it? After tossing the elements into the air like straw in the winds they did indeed settle into regular patterns.

67. Sketch exterior of second Rucker house - April 9, 1971

The final solution accommodated our best views to the south and east and remained within the ninety feet square property allowances. We used the twenty-six and a half feet-square foundations with the caissons and steel column posts on the corners as the main structural support and were able to accommodate cars arriving and leaving within the limited space. For aerodynamic reasons we kept the lines of the house smooth so it would be unable to catch flying sparks, and rather than raising the whole house one story above the motor court as in the previously house, we decided to put living quarters on the motor court level and go downstairs

A Tale of Two Houses

to the four small bedrooms beneath. We kept the circular stairway because it saved space and we enjoyed walking up and down with no intermediate landing to slow us down.

Steve, Lew, Richard Sol, structural engineer, David Weiss and I completed the working drawings on October 17, 1971 and they were submitted to the building department before the end of November, 1971. We signed a contract with Roy Norvelle on October first, 1971, and it is interesting to note labor rates based on a Union scale:

Forman	7.53 per hour
Carpenter	6.93 per hour
First year carpenter	4.16 per hour
Health and Welfare	.61 per hour
Pension	.75 per hour
Vacation pay	.55 per hour
Apprenticeship	.01 per hour

15.5% of total hourly wage was added to pay for workmen's compensation and public liability insurance and property damage. For a seasoned carpenter, Norvelle would be charging 6.93 + .61 + .75 + .55 + 01 or *$8.85 per hour.*

I'm continually surprised that a general contractor can ask twenty or thirty of his subs to estimate their work, guess his own time to complete the job, charge according to the type of life he wants to live, add an amount for things he forgot or unforeseen troubles and still become the low bidder and get the job.

We'd start construction the first week in January 1972.

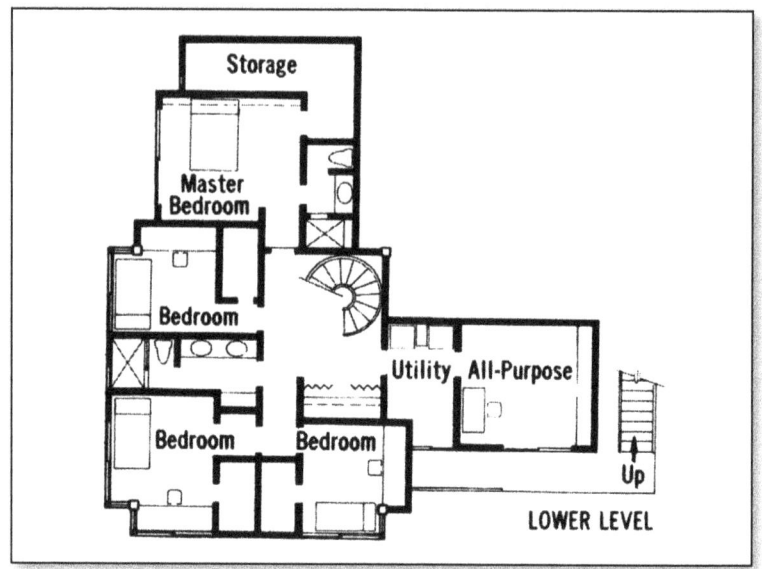

68. Lower floor of second Rucker house.

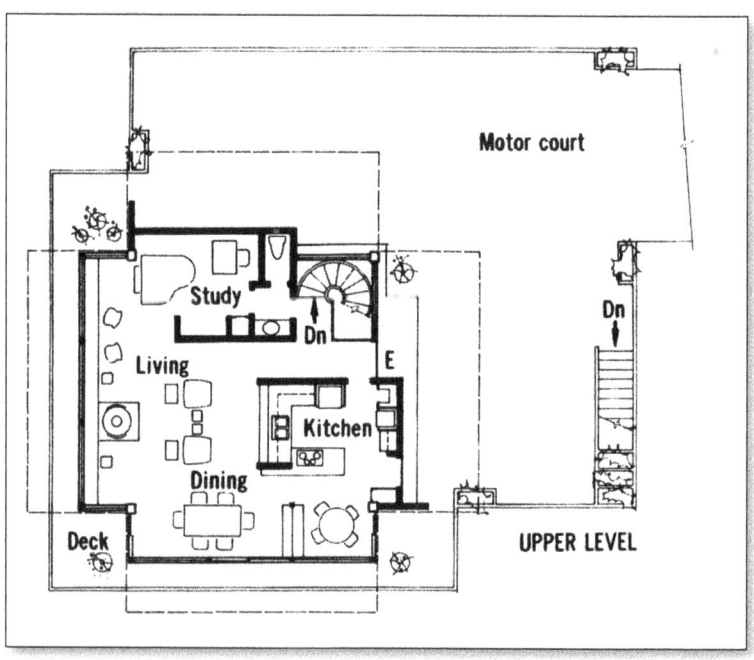

69. Upper floor of second Rucker house.

A Tale of Two Houses

MALIBU TIMES ARTICLE - December 3, 1971

The "Big Barn" at 22971 Pacific Coast Highway is fast becoming a true artist's colony for Malibu. History of the "barn" reveals the original private railroad station of Mrs. Rhoda (sic) Rindge in her fight to keep commercial trains off her domain; for many years a lumber yard - today it houses businesses such as Perfect Glass & Mirror, Malibu TV Cable Service, and Architect Douglas Rucker. But the front door leads into the Gallery Book & Art Supply operated by Teresa White; Fayrene Parrish, sculptress, and the latest addition is the Christmas Gift Boutique with handcrafted articles collected from east to west - including Malibu.

OVAL MEDALLION

70. Oval window decoration.

In the *"old Rindge barn"* sharing a wall and to the east of my studio was an antique store, perhaps twenty feet wide and forty feet deep. The owners were a friendly and compatible family consisting, I think, of a middle-aged man and his wife and a son-in-law or nephew. Their seventeen-century items were mostly shipped by boat from Scotland. When I came to visit through their garage door size opening, I noticed ancient couches, chairs, desks, tables, armoires, and the like for sale.

71. Doug at work next to his window.

Through narrow isles and deeper within was storage of large unfinished furniture and at the very rear a table and oils and stains for refinishing. Considering old chairs, the husband jokingly commented, *"There's an ass for every seat."* I've forgotten the names of these interesting Scottish people, but came across a window decoration I couldn't do without.

RUCKER HOUSE NUMBER 2

Many months ago Karon and I had hired a clean-up crew to haul away ashes, steel, and burned construction of the pedestal house. The site was neat except for weedy volunteers alongside still usable foundations. Friend and Structural Engineer, David Weiss, had inspected the footings long ago and did *not* find them wanting. Four caissons yet remained laid out at the corners of a perfect twenty-five foot-six-inch square foundation. There were still four thick caissons reaching down twelve feet expanding into eight-foot diameter bells bearing directly on firm soil. Fire damage for the caissons was impossible as it was for half-buried concrete grade beams asserting their identity through green weeds. They remained strongly united caisson tops.

Roy Norvelle and I walked the site preparatory to rebuilding early in 1972. When the heavy tube-steel columns had collapsed during the fire and a portion of a corner of a grade beam under the steel base plate had sloughed off, I wondered if it had weakened the connection. Upon inspection, the foundation bolts were still well buried in the grade beam and more than sufficiently strong to hold new loads. The nick in the exposed grade beam was merely unsightly and could be repaired with forms and bolts drilled into the existing concrete and a small pour.

Roy made his lumber list and ordered four-foot by eight-foot by three-quarter-inch plywood for floors and ceiling, two-by-six studs for walls and a quantity of twenty-four-inch and thirty-six-inch deep truss joists. While lumber was on order Roy's men hand-dug a few new trenches, formed, drilled and placed the new foundation bolts and hold-downs, then poured minor supports preparatory to framing.

WORKING ON THE JOB

Quitting my architectural day at 5:30 PM, I went home, changed into T-shirt, Levi's, and work boots and drove to our site to work as a laborer to move along our insufficiently funded job. Because lumber trucks couldn't negotiate our steep driveway, plywood had to be delivered and dumped on a neighbor's empty pad slightly downhill and a hundred yards away. I got permission from our generous neighbor and with bandana tied tightly around my forehead under a baseball cap, I donned gloves and tried walking two three-quarter-inch thick plywood panels at a time. I was going to carry a hundred or more pieces of plywood along a narrow dirt pathway three hundred feet uphill and deposit it into a pile at the motor court level.

Lifting two panels over my shoulder and with another heave, I hoisted them onto my head, and carefully balancing, step by step, made my way along the dirt pathway. I made four trips before deciding they were too heavy and faced the fact that carrying one at a time it would take twice as long as expected. For a couple of hours each day I labored with the panels until my task was completed. I'd now lift one three-quarter-inch panel, set it on my head, and walk uphill the hundred yards to the new pile, stop; thank God I'd made it, and return to pick up the next. Resting while walking back, I'd balance the next panel and trudge again upslope.

72. *Amanda and Lilianne on neighbor's pad.*
Note winding pathway uphill to job site.

Since carrying three-quarter-inch plywood sheets required little thought, I had time to ponder other things and feel and enjoy the effort of applying formerly sedentary muscles to a useful project. The crisp horizon met my eye with delight and I was intoxicated with fresh westerly winds and frequently the pink, gray and white clouds and setting sun were awesome. At age forty-five, heavy labor suited me.

I accepted the challenge and worked with enthusiasm and anticipation. I was rebuilding my burned house! I'd designed it! I'd got the permit and was doing it! I was reliving my California proxy architect brother, Rick's and my philosophy, *"Looketh not at what he SAYETH he goin' to do, but looketh, rather, at what he already DONE DO."* I had not only *said* I was going to rebuild a new house, but I was *on the path, hauling wood and doing it!* I slept well those nights.

73. *Delivering steel columns.*

74. *Installing first column.*

75. Column installation.

76. Roy Norvelle supervising.

77. Placing a steel beam.

78. Setting easterly facing steel beams.

79. Crane lifting the 49'-6" x 3'-0" truss joists into place.

80. Placing intersecting truss joists.

After doing minor foundation work, contractor Roy Norvelle, had his men do as much wood framing as possible largely to determine the exact positions of steel columns and framework. Since placement of columns and truss joists required a crane, Roy was prepared with stored material to do both.

Placing four, forty-nine-feet-six-inch by thirty-six-inch-deep intersecting truss joists was next. To support the roof, four large truss joists measuring almost fifty-feet long were to intersect each other at the four corners over the heavy tube-steel columns; two truss joists running north and south and two truss joists east and west. Not only that but the two east-west facing beams were to be 1/2 truss lower than the two north-south facing.

I have highest praise for Norvelle's professional framer, whose name unfortunately I've forgotten, who continued the rough framing well past the complicated lifting of the main truss joists into place.

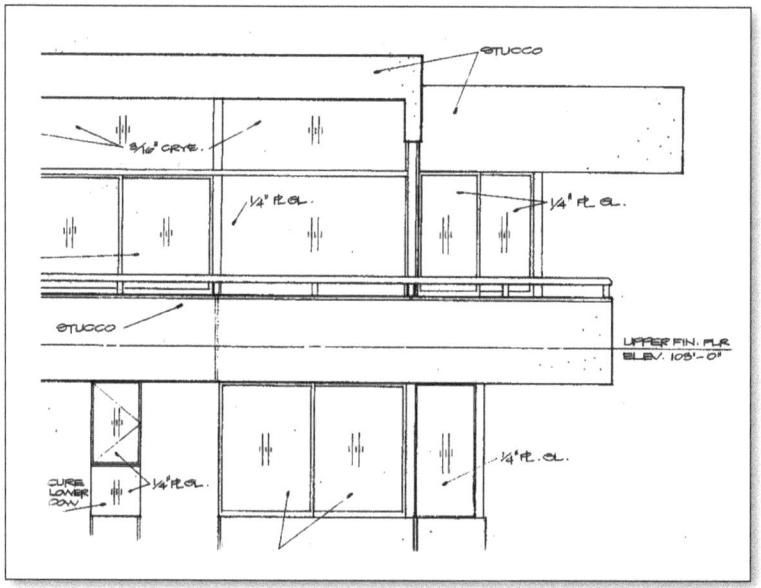

81. A Working drawing showing truss joist intersection.

82. *Intersecting the next corner.*

83. Setting the fourth truss joist.

84. From above

85. Northwest side.

86. Southeast side.

87. From west side.

88. North side from above.

Trial By Fire - *Doug Rucker*

BIRTH OF A HOUSE

On August 7, 1972 Santa Monica's Evening Outlook published an article by staff writer, Kit Cowdrey, with photographs about our second Malibu house called:

From the ashes

BIRTH OF A HOUSE

Doug recalls: "The new Malibu home of the Doug Rucker family is almost ready for occupancy. After we lost our home in the September 1970 fire, the prospect of designing a new house and moving back on the same site was so painful we spent about six months considering other alternatives, mainly looking at houses to buy." *None of the houses they looked at suited the family's life style, which includes many interests and activities. Doug, an architect, supervises the construction as well as drawing plans for his clients. Between designing new homes for about a dozen Malibu residents (some had lost their homes in the fire), the architect redesigned a new home for his family.*

The family includes his wife, Karon; three daughters, Vivi, 11, Lili, 10, and Mandy, 7; two Siamese cats named Yum Yum and Nanki Poo, and Daisy, a black and white terrier. Doug thinks the new house is much more tied to the landscape than the other house, and is perched on a square pedestal.

"We think it's as fireproof as possible. It's plastered down to the ground and entirely of plaster and glass with very little exposure of the under-floor area. It could be called California Contemporary.

We have four bedrooms ... each girl has her own room. There's a kitchen, dining, living room combination, a den-guest room, a sewing alcove, a crafts room for Karon, and a shop-studio for me."

A Tale of Two Houses

89. First Malibu family home built by architect, Doug Rucker. (Razed in 1970 fire.)

90. Doug Rucker is building a new home on the same site as the first home. View from Pacific Coast Highway.

91. At picnic lunch break in Rucker's new living-dining room area grandmother Mrs. Herman Conan peels an avocado for sandwiches for Doug, Mandy 7, Mother Karon, Vivi 11, and Lili 10.

 The house has a built-in vacuum cleaner system. All the closets are walk-in "...so if the girls drop clothes on the floor when they change, we can just close the door."
 Because for two years the family has lived in the close quarters of a two-bedroom apartment, Doug has provided built-in privacy for all members. There is a double walk-in closet between Vivi and Mandy's room, and a sound insulated wall between Lili's room and the master bedroom.
 The quietest room is Karon's crafts room. She teaches crafts at Carden and Webster School and at her own studio, "Variations on a Thread," in the Malibu Art Colony building. (Former Rindge railroad terminal and later, barn.) Another quiet room is Doug's shop beside his studio where he plans to do his writing, drafting and painting. (He lost 60 paintings in the fire.)

92. Mandy Rucker, 7, stretches from banister of stairwell to first level of her new home.

"The piano will be there, too. Karon and I belong to two musical groups, the Meister Singers and the Neo Renaissance Singers." As in their other house, every window has a view where the Rucker's can follow the moods of ocean and canyon and the geranium gardens along the highway.

"We have learned much from losing a home," Karon says. "After the fire we still had the things we'd given away, like Doug's drawings. But we didn't have the things we kept."

"The tragedy is losing things you can't recreate, like the pictures of our children, letters and family heirlooms. But if you're used to creating things, the wonderful thing is the process of doing, not the process of keeping."

CONDOMINIUM MOVE

On the first of July, Roy Norvelle and I selected a cabinet man and stucco contractor. A week later stucco material was delivered to the job and work began. The new condominium owner's furniture was to arrive on July 20th and we were to stay with it for a few weeks until they took permanent possession on September 1st. We expected to move into our partially completed house a week or so earlier and no later than August 22nd but our house wasn't done and we actually moved into the Halpin's guest room on August 15th making room for the new owners on August 19th. The Halpin's were former clients of mine and I was fortunate to design their now completed house after the fire.

At the end of August the following remained to be done; finished cabinetwork and appliances, tile floor, tile counter tops, plumbing fixtures, heat registers, glazing, lighting, carpeting, finish carpentry work, metal fireplace installation and painting and staining, Our moving-in estimate was about the middle of November, six weeks later than expected. We were far too optimistic.

Letter excerpt - August 26, 1972
To Mother and Dad,
… There is tons of work to do around the house and I don't nearly have the time to do it all. As I've mentioned, the house is running about $10,000.00 over what we expected.
… The house job has been more or less dead for the last ten days because we need scaffolding to reach the sides and eaves of the house with the plastering hose.
… The scaffolding contractors are loaded up weeks in advance. Our job is a small one but difficult and not the type for a scaffolding contractor to make a fast buck on, and so we wait and fume and brood. I'm so anxious to get back in our new house I'm beside myself. Anyway, I'll try to keep you posted on the progress. What we are going to do for a place to live for a month or so while our house is being finished, I don't know. Something will no doubt turn up. Anyway, as you can see, vacation thoughts must come secondary. We have to get out of this mess and settled before we can lead a more normal life.
Love, Doug

Letter excerpt – No Date
Mother and Dad,
… The house is progressing, but still very slowly. We finally got over the scaffolding and we are now into the plastering stage.

A Tale of Two Houses

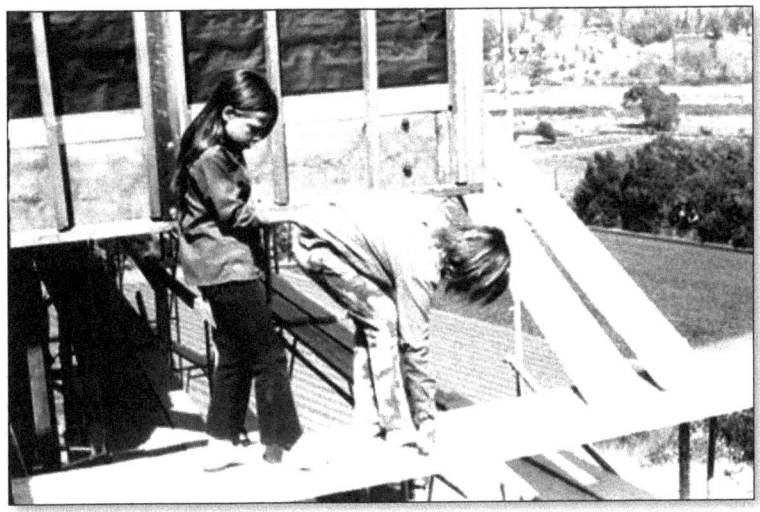

93. Lili and Vivi on scaffolding.

The plastering, however, is going in fits and starts, which is frustrating and nerve-wracking when you are in an anxious state, as we are. I think the various stages are up to go fairly quickly. After plastering comes. (a) cabinetwork and appliances, (b) tile work on floor and counter tops, (c) plumbing fixture installation, (d) lighting fixture installation, (e) carpeting and flooring, (f) glazing and carpentry work done simultaneously with other work, (g) metal fireplace installation. So, who knows - say six weeks before we can move in and camp out?

Speaking of camping out. The new owner of our condominium unit, Andrew Stedry, arrived last Tuesday and began his occupancy of his new unit. The week previous was hectic and indescribable. We had to move two years of accumulated stuff out of our apartment unit. Half the stuff we boxed and stuck under the house. The other half we took to our new place of residence - the Halpin's new house.

About a year before, I started designs on Eugene and Virginia Lee Halpin's new home. Part of the program was to provide guest quarters on the lower floor. It consisted of a small room, ten by thirteen-feet, a small bath with tub-shower, a six-foot kitchen cabinet and a niche for a refrigerator. Little did I know our family was to be the Halpin's first guests? Karon and I occupied the guest quarters and a tent accommodated the three kids, a dog and two cats. We had our sofa bed against one wall, chairs and settee here and there, books and lamps and a TV set.

94. Mandy, Lil, Doug, Viv in front of tent.

Letter – No Date
Dear Mother and Dad,

We seem to be adjusting OK to the rather cramped quarters. Being in less space means we have less junk to deal with. I really believe in traveling light. Also, we do not have a home phone right now and are more or less not accessible to the outside world. I feel I can go home now and not be accessible to people's problems. It's like being on vacation. The tent is large – eight-feet by ten-feet with two large screened strip-windows each end and a big entry door so you can be inside, look out and feel the breeze. The three children seem to like it out there under the trees. I've slept out there a couple of times and it was really great. Last night Mandy had a guest over - Megan Dixon - who is built solid, like Mandy and they are two peas in a pod. They've been running and chasing each other all over the place. It is great to see them because they are so joyful together.

Please be in good health, Doug

Letter excerpts - September 9, 1972
Dear Mother and Dad,

(a) We are building a house that takes time and requires a drain on the finances.

(b) The kids have been home all summer from school and, though we love 'em, they do take up time. Lessons, etc.

(c) We are living in one room with three kids in a tent plus two cats and a dog and no cooking facilities except a hot plate and a hibachi.

(d) Business has been good. I have five jobs under construction, two ready to begin and five ready for drawings with only a student helping me.

(e) Karon is becoming a women's libber and while I agree she should, I do not have the "I'll take care of you" type of wife.

These are a few of the reasons I don't have too many spare moments. Even so, we manage to sing with the Renaissance Singers once a week and our other group, The

Malibu Meistersingers, will be starting in two weeks. I still take Vivi to her springboard diving lessons twice a week. (I dive too.) I take Lili to her piano lesson once a week. Karon takes Vivi to guitar lessons once a week. All three kids go to crocheting lessons once or twice a week.

I go running everyday and I swear it is conditioning to keep up the pace of this Southern California life. By the way, recently I've been going about three-miles a day averaging seven minutes per mile and am down to 155 pounds in the morning now. Being in good running and physical condition with running and springboard diving gymnastics makes me feel really great. I am also eating the right foods, too, laying off junk like chocolate and alcohol. So, though our schedule is filled up minute to minute, we seem to have a full, rich life. It may be a fuller and richer life than most people, but it takes more energy to live. I feel we are living to the fullest in the present moments and though our schedule is filled to the brim, we nevertheless seem to thrive on the activities and interesting things to do in this locale.

One thing that would be beneficial to us would be a month's rest somewhere - a kind of breather before we get back in the swim of living.

Let me digress for a moment. About two weeks ago, I went jogging with our family doctor, Dr. John Heiken, who is about forty-three and in better physical condition than I am. We went about four miles and I finished a full two minutes after he finished. When I finally arrived back at his office he already had the blood pressure apparatus out and was taking his own blood pressure. He asked if I would like to have mine checked "while he had it out?" I agreed and we checked it at three and five minute intervals. (It takes me 28 minutes to run four miles.)

Immediately after the run it was 190/80. Five minutes later it was 156/84. Five minutes later it was 136/86. So in approximately ten minutes after an exhaustive run I *obtained the lowest blood pressure figure I've had since I can remember. Also, that run was over twice as far as I'd been used to going and I just barely finished it with guts and will power. Since then I've been running three miles a day. Today I went five. So, in a few months the effort to run four miles won't be as great as it was that first time with Dr. Heiken.*

95. Dr. John Heiken and Doug at later 10K race.

96. Doug with new Pepperdine University in the west.

Letter excerpts - October 22, 1972
Dear Mother and Dad,
… The house is lumping along as usual. That is, things are progressing slowly. Right now what's happening is:
    1 We are cleaning up after the plasterers.
    2 We are beginning painting and staining.
    3 Carpenters are doing finish work.
    4 Glass is to begin going in this week.
    5 Tile is going in this week. It will take two weeks and we must wait for this to be finished before we can start putting in our toilet, appliances, and electrical fixtures.
    Everything is costing an arm and a leg and it looks like we'll have to borrow money to get the job finished. It was ever thus. Hope it doesn't burn down again. Love, Doug.

A Tale of Two Houses

Continuing letter excerpts - October 24, 1972

...We are starting to "bug" the people we are staying with. This morning Karon picked up the phone to call the school on Vivi's behalf and Mrs. Halpin was on the line upstairs. She said, "Would you PLEASE get off the line!" I was tempted to move out today, but over three quarters of the floors in our house will be torn up while they're laying floor tile. The plumbing fixtures can't be set until the floor tile is down. It will take two weeks from next Thursday to get the floor tile in place and so what are we supposed to do, move all our stuff to a motel for two weeks? I might as well quit work with all that moving. It's hard to be a guest for too long. Unfortunately, it's also impossible to leave and so we are going to continue to endure the situation. We're not completely guests, since I'm paying them $200.00 a month for rent.

The cats are in a four-foot by eight-foot cage thats only three and a half-feet high and don't like it. They poop all over and smell it up. Mrs. Halpin doesn't like it either.

97. Mandy with beloved, night barking Daisy.

The dog, Daisy, also loves to charge out into the night and bark at owls, birds, other dogs, and just for the fun of it. Mrs. Halpin doesn't like that either.

I shouldn't paint too poor a picture of her since I'm sure you can see her side of it. She does love the house I designed for her and has been a tremendous booster for me in the past. I just want to get out in time to save the good relationship I (we) have.

Letter excerpts - November 4, 1972
Dear Mother and Dad,
Well, here I am again at the Laundromat washing for a family of five. Lili is at her lesson and, where I used to relax and write letters to you and just rest while she was playing, now I have to use this "relax time" to do the laundry. Things are looking up, though. We are going to move in our new house on the fifteenth of this month, whatever is there! Even those prospects look good now, though.

The plasterer finally finished his work. The scaffolding blew down in a high wind and left large, permanent and unsightly scratches high on the side of the building. It has now been picked up. The glass and glazing is three quarters completed. The tile men have done the kitchen and pullman cabinets and are starting the lower floor quarry tile. The electrical man was to begin his finish work today and the plumber will be setting a toilet, wash basin and shower and hooking up the furnace and water heater Monday. Also the carpenters are doing final finishing work and building the stairway to the lower floor (outside) from the motor court deck. The sheet metal man will have our outdoor planter box inserts next week, etc., etc. This weekend Karon and I and two laborers will be beginning our painting and finishing work. I have already designed us a dining room table and it is in my office ready to be finished and put to use though we still have no chairs yet.

98. Vivi waving at Dad from the window of her new room.

Lois Conan did come up with some nice looking - turn-of-the-century furniture, though. She gave us a treadle type sewing machine in perfect condition that Karon may make over into a spinning wheel. How is beyond me, but if anyone can, she can. Also, she gave us a couple of old interesting chairs and a rocker. We have our "fire" gifts of beds for the kids, but Karon and I do not have a bed. It is my plan to design us one and have it made. Maybe Harry Heckendorf could do it.   *See you. Love, Doug*

NEW HOUSE

Having moved in the Halpin's on August 15th with hot plate, cat cage, nighttime barking dog and our bed in a tiny room with a tent-for-daughters under the trees, we thought we'd only be there a month. We were actually there three months leaving on November 15th. Not many letters were written since November 9th, but I found one around the first of December.

Letter excerpts – December 1, 1972
Dear Mother and Dad
… We have been moving in our house for the past two weeks and so things are upset, but exciting just the same. Cleaning up after the workmen seems unending. As of today we have everything in working order, except …

(a) The glass man has to install three sliding glass doors now boarded up.
(b) Carpets have to go in.
(c) Built-in desks for the kids must be installed.
(d) We have no bed.

We have things workable like our washer dryer, dishwasher, heat unit and water heater and are painting and finishing now.

The kids are overjoyed at last to have a room all their own, and we feel so good spreading out after having lived in a ten-by-fourteen room with three kids in a tent and two cats in a cage for so long.

Sunday I washed the windows and the view is just marvelous. You must come visit us this Christmas. Just think, that's just four weeks away. Better start planning now. What day for your arrival would be convenient for you? You will sleep in Vivi's room and Vivi will move into the "library".

(Karon's new crafts room.)

My office work seems to be holding up just fine except that Malibu is going through some growing pains. There is a building freeze at the moment that creates lots of extra work for me, since I have to expedite my work through additional bureaucratic agencies.

Must quit. We are all fine here. We think of you often. Love, Doug

99. From the southwest.

Trial By Fire - *Doug Rucker*

100. Three quarter view.

RESUMING LIFE

Or, should I say, *"Our life continued its fateful course."* We did the next thing! Our pedestal house burned on September 25, 1970 and in slightly over two years we occupied a new house on the first of December, 1972. In the meantime the world had moved forward a few notches and we had moved with it. We were two years older. We were smarter. We'd had new experiences. When the house burned, our daughters were six, eight and ten. Now they were eight, ten and twelve. Viveka, was doing well in the former Malibu Park Junior High School on Morning View Drive. Lili and Mandy were in third and fifth grades at Webster Elementary School. Karon was teaching crafts at Webster and minding

A Tale of Two Houses

children after school. None of the children had stopped their lessons. I was inundated with work. Karon's parents, Lois and Duke Conan, had returned from Mountain Home, Arkansas and living in Point Dume Mobile Home Park. As much as we would have liked my parents, Eva and Phil, here for Christmas, it was not to be. I suspect they wanted to give us time to become accustomed to life in our new house.

In some fashion we had Christmas in the new house. I presume we had a tree and gifts, dinner with Duke and Lois, and that I took time off. There was the short, vacation week to my 45th birthday on New Years Eve and new years day. On January 4th, we celebrated Karon's 41st birthday and were probably tired of so many celebrations, but at least we'd made it through 1972 to the beginning of 1973.

Letter excerpts - March 22, 1973
Dear Mother and Dad,
...Vivi had to get glasses last week and looks a little different to us all. You won't recognize her. ...We have three good kids and you'll be proud of them when you see them. I also drove Lili to her piano lesson, trading off now and then with Karon.

We were in a concert at the Santa Monica Methodist Church singing Laud to the Nativity by Respighi, a beautiful piece for chorus, soloists and string orchestra. On the same program we sang Benjamin Britten's, Rejoice in the Lamb and Johannes Brahms Liebisleider Waltzes. Brahms wrote nineteen waltzes and we did six of them. I quote from an old letter, "They are love songs and I have never been so exhilarated over singing music. After the concert I was on top of the world. The music is fantastic and the idea of love songs is even better. Brahms is a real master."

A new member of the Malibu Meistersinger group, Dave Rodriguez, has agreed to pay for moving his mother's baby Steinway piano from Santa Monica to be stored freely in our house for an unspecified time. Lili's thrilled!

Though Karon seemed ambivalent toward our pedestal house, I was gratified she thought the new house was a joy. She was weaving and teaching crafts at Webster Elementary. The children were healthy, popular in school, and seemed to be enjoying life. I felt like a lucky guy; it was so much fun to watch them grow. I thought in another ten years they'll be gone and I'll miss them, but Karon and I consoled ourselves that we'd have activities and were thinking of traveling in later life when our children have moved to their next phase.

While writing to mother I was explaining our example of frugality.

Except for the cost of our new house and lessons for our kids, our family has no economic vices; we don't' go out to dinner, we don't' drink, we don't throw big parties, we don't go to plays, operas, football games, etc., we don't buy fancy clothes. (My daily work clothes are two-year old corduroys and a sweatshirt.) We did go out on a limb for long-term benefits by getting tile floors and a good grade of carpet, windows and glass.

Cousin, Gene Kennard, dropped by with his family and when I took him below the house, he looked up and said, "Well, it doesn't have the drama of the last house, does it?" He was clearly not "sent" by the house, but doesn't see it as we do. While lukewarm on the former house, Karon loves our new house, which is gratifying to me. Her liking the house made my life simpler. Where the other was "tense" and tentative, the new house has strength and solidity. It's much quieter, more solid and accommodates our family with better privacy. It also has the potential for growth and should get better with time. Last week we rode out a 5.5 earthquake with the epicenter in the ocean off Oxnard. Not a thing fell off shelves and no cracks were found anywhere. It would appear the house is built solidly.

…We will be doing the annual Pleasure Faire in

Calabasas again this year. They will be holding it for six weekends which will be the longest ever. The kids always have a good time for it is a colorful and entertaining event. We will be singing all the old repertoire madrigals that we practically know by heart. We were working on the William Byrd Mass for October.
Love, Doug

RUNNING

I was running one or two miles a day and my heartbeat was down to about forty-eight in the morning and sixty in the afternoon and one-hundred-twenty to one-hundred-thirty during fast running. I felt healthy and had no heart palpitations as I had in the pedestal house. So the combination of a slightly more secure practice, minimum anxiety in my home life, daily exercise of mind and body and staying reasonably slim brought about a good mental and physical condition I hoped would develop into a lifetime habit.

I'd been reading a good article in the National Geographic on aging and people in the world over one hundred years old. The oldest living man was one-hundred-and-sixty-seven years old and there were many a hundred to a hundred-thirty. A couple of facts: there were no obese centurions and all those interviewed led tough physical lives including work that required lots of walking, leg action and huffing and puffing. The group studied most were married doing useful work, enjoying life and were mentally bright.

OFFICE LIFE

In the office, there was greater difficulty in getting permits for my clients and costs continued to rise but in spite of the building moratorium, business was going well. At this time three or four other architects were doing business in Malibu and I was doing a far greater quantity of work than any of the others. While the octagon house was being completed, the Dixon's and their children, Pahl, seventeen, Jamie, twelve and Megan, eight, became close friends.

The twenty-four-hundred square foot Munro house was beginning construction and I was doing preliminaries for a four-thousand-square-foot house for Ruth and Judge Ed Rafeedie. Our hoped-for budget was $110,000.00. I was doing a preliminary for a member of our Neo Renaissance singing group, Charlene Heacock, and a new small house for Jeff and Bunny Terrill in Monte Nido.

Though draftsman, Lew Dominy and Steve Wooley had left my office, Rick Davidson was back and I had a young graduate from S.C. just learning, but hope he will become useful in a few months. (Regretfully, he did not.)

LOS ANGELES TIMES

In April of 1973 I got a welcome letter from Dan McMasters, Los Angeles Times Home magazine editor. I was pleased Dan wanted to publish my house; in fact I always hoped he would. In business, one essential method by which you can get people to know your name and work, is to advertise. Ted Turner's father proposed a motto, *"Early to bed, early to rise, do your work and advertise."* Not only was my not-too-timid-ego electrified by the letter, but it was my sincerest hope more publicity would bring more work. Concerning work, all I could think of was *"more, more, more."* I could handle any quantity of design work as long as I had the means to get it into three dimensions. I held visions of my wonderful buildings bringing tears of joy to thousands of people. *(One of my poems: Ego as big as the whole outdoors. Over the canyon rim it soars.)* I informed him I thought a publication would be delightful and accepted the fact that a press announcement would take time. It took months before the house was photographed and the article was published.

This time Glen Allison did the photography and I was

unhappy I was not his assistant because he'd brought his own. Glen photographed, I waited, waited, waited and months later on that magic day of August 11, 1974 the sun rose and brought forth my beloved article.

PUBLICATION

On the cover of the Los Angeles Times Homes section a caption read, *"A Tale of Two Houses and a Trial by Fire."*
Under a picture of the living room interior taken from the deck by Los Angeles Times photographer, Glenn Allison, the underlying caption read,

"This is the tale of two houses, one that burned in the great Malibu Mountains fire and the other - shown here - that rose from the ashes on the same site. Both were designed by Doug Rucker for his family. Rucker wrote in the Home magazine in 1970 of the fire. Here he tells what it means to lose everything - except those things that mean most - and how he planned his new house to survive another holocaust."

Then a copy of what I'd written as published in the Home section on August 11, 1974 with the title:

"THE HOUSE THAT ROSE FROM THE ASHES."
By Douglas Rucker.

During the early days after the fire, we really didn't fully understand what had happened. There was so much to do, getting the children back into their school routine, setting up an office, getting identification papers in order. When you lose your birth certificate, marriage and drivers licenses, insurance and tax records and grocery card, it is difficult to prove you exist. We remember most falling into bed exhausted late at night.

101. House on cover of Los Angeles Times Home magazine.

Volunteer disaster centers had sprung up immediately to receive and disperse shoes, pants, coats, sweaters, etc., in every conceivable size and shape to aid forty or so families who lost their homes. We accepted (and) were gratefully amazed. A close friend came to our rescue with temporary housing, rent-free, in her two-room, over-the-garage walk-

up in the Malibu Colony. It was cramped for a family of five but we managed by folding up the dining room table and unfolding the sofa bed at night and doing the reverse in the morning.

102. Living room.

Another close friend helped solve my office problem by donating office space next to his art store on Pacific Coast

Highway. It had been a potter's studio and the clay was two inches thick everywhere. One day a carpenter friend (Fritz Schafer) appeared to build me an entrance. Another friend donated two weeks finishing out a fine, though necessarily modest, architectural office. Concerned architects gave me drafting equipment; soon I had a simple but attractive and workable establishment.

One friend, belatedly hearing of our loss, offered me "anything." I said, "Thanks, I need a can of rubber cement." Many, many friends reached to us from all sides and kept us aloft. In fact, we were so buoyed up by friends it became almost an obligation not to lose heart or give way.

Other fire victims who wanted to rebuild knew that I would understand their special problems and so rather quickly business returned. Soon I had to put on a draftsman to help with my workload, then another. I became so absorbed in rebuilding other homes and my wife was so absorbed in teaching crafts and home activities, that months passed before we gave a thought to rebuilding our own home. Finally, we came to realize we must seek a more permanent housing solution for ourselves. But this time we would pursue the simple life.

One of our feelings immediately after the fire was that of intense relief. We hadn't realized that possessions are a responsibility and sometimes possess the possessor. You must use them, care for them, maintain them and insure them (we didn't). The fire relieved us of that responsibility. Now we could go anywhere or do anything. We thought of moving to romantic islands, with sun-browned, if uneducated, children on the sand. We thought of selling our lot and buying farmland in Agoura and being self-sufficient. How wonderful to be free.

This Walter Mitty state of mind lasted a month or so, until the grim, immediate necessities descended upon us and made us consider things like, "How will we get food for tonight?" and "Where will our way of life be - that part we

A Tale of Two Houses

enjoyed?" We soon decided that Malibu was pretty great after all and had about all we ever would need.

At first, the thought of rebuilding on the same site was distasteful because we linked it with tragedy. We would buy an existing house and adapt it to our needs. We searched for about three months and found that places we could afford we didn't like, and the places we liked we couldn't afford. For economical and self-image reasons we decided we must build on the same site. Even on the same foundations.

103. House from above showing ocean, Surfrider Beach and wide expanse of geranium gardens.

Once the decision to rebuild was made, what to build became the big question. What house should replace our passionate wood, glass and steel palace we had worked so hard for, and had loved and lost?

After all, we owned the lot free and clear. Our assets amounted to a lot with a paved road and utilities stubbed out to the debris. We also had an intact private sewage-disposal system. That was it - not bad for a start.

We wanted to try something different. This should be a new kind of house, but simpler, for our new lifestyle. For economies sake, it would be constructed exactly over the existing footings. This would be limiting to the design but also a challenge. Its materials would be concrete, stucco and glass, fire-resistant to weather some future brush fire. It would also extend to the ground with no openings to invite the wind and fire. It would be embarrassing for an architect's home to burn down twice in the same place in front of everybody.

104. Kitchen and children's breakfast counter.

Also, it should nestle into the hillside. Our former pedestal-type house perched on the hill was vulnerable to the elements. A lower, heavier house would be more stable in the strong Santa Ana winds. This time, instead of the entire house being on one floor, the living quarters would be on the motor court level and bedrooms downstairs.

Karon had no trouble agreeing on the basic design but fought tooth and nail for the details. After many hours of discussion and lots of compromise, we arrived at a design we both liked - one that would minimize the fire hazards and allow our family to function gracefully, as far as possible with three lively daughters.

105. House from below & southeast.

We completed the plans, selected Roy J. Norvelle as our contractor and began. It had been one full year since the fire. It would be another full year before completion. Twenty-one months were spent in a two-bedroom Malibu condominium. When our lease was up and we were forced *to move, we accepted another generous offer to stay with friends in their guest room for what we thought would be two weeks. Construction took longer. Karon and I shared the guest room and the children shared an eight-by-ten-foot tent outside under a tree for nine weeks. This experience was memorable, but our family and friends did survive.*

106. Living-dining area looking southwest.

Late in November of 1972 we brought our first load of belongings down the hill to the new house. What a thrill. Thanksgiving in our own house! And what a great feeling to know that we would no longer impose on our friends. It is difficult to stay on the receiving end for such a long time. We would be independent again. Daisy, our dog, ran all over the hillside investigating everything.

Our daughters, Vivi, Lili, and Mandy could go into their own rooms and be alone for the first time in two years. Ironically, they were lonely for one another for the first few weeks. We're still amazed at the extent to which our friends helped us. We learned that losing one's possessions does not mean the end of life, nor does it even change one's *essential way of life.*

107. Living room from exterior deck.

Looking back, it seems an inner force compelled us to rebuild and try to do a better job. But the most valuable thing we learned was that without good health, intact family and good friends, the recuperation would have been very difficult. They were the heart that pumped courage into our efforts.

We appreciate our home doubly now, having done it twice. How many architects' get a second chance?

SOL AND ANOTHER HOME TOUR

My friend and draftsman, Richard Sol, a traveling scholarship winner from Southern California University, was on an important AIA committee and notified me that, again, the Southern California AIA was looking for homes to tour in Malibu. He thought of me and seemed to know our new house was something that would appeal to the AIA. We were contacted and this time Karon recognized the publicity advantage of being on the tour. A time was set and the tour, like the former, happened. I was flattered and delighted.

108. House seen from adjacent lot.

FINAL SALUTE

I assume, because the house was so visible from the highway, and both houses were so different in appearance than others being built, the Rucker House was selected by Gebhardt and Winter to be in their book, a *Los Angeles Guide to Architecture*. I was particularly delighted with this selection because it put my name with other architects whom I admired, Frank Lloyd Wright, Richard Neutra, Quincy Jones, John Lautner and others who'd made significant architectural contributions to Southern California and the world. When I saw my name in print I became aware that possibly I had also made a significant contribution. I considered my architectural life worth it, for here was my claim to fame.

109. House from below.

A LITTLE BIT OF AFTERWARD

In our first few years in our second new house we strove for normalcy. Between raising a family with a dog and two cats and sometimes sheep, we painted, made shelving, did brush clearance, landscaped and built a room for tool storage, all while working full-time. Eventually, new furniture was acquired, paintings were hung, a baby-grand piano was borrowed and we entered more rationally into the next phase of our lives. At eight, ten and twelve, the children went back to Webster Elementary School. They studied and became good students and outstanding singers performing in Webster's Madrigal Group and winning prizes in the L. A. County solo competitions. Entering puberty in Malibu's difficult 1970's period, both parents and young adults had their work cut out for them. For a while, Karon was passionately involved in hand-weaving wool. We obtained two sheep that unfortunately ended in tragedy. One hung itself on its own chain and the other succumbed to coyotes. We learned a shameful lesson. Soon to become her medium of choice, Karon had begun making large, exceptional art works out of colored electrical wire. Architecturally, I was busy enough to keep Toby Watson and hire a diligent new draftsman from Cal Poly in San Luis Obisbo named Niel Dilworth. My work was mostly in Malibu, but I also did a house on Kauai's northeast shore and remodelled a two-hundred-year-old house in Greece on the Island of Korfu. But the rest of what happened after the fire is another story. Now, I'm living in the Malibu hills with my lovely wife, Marge. She's continuing her artwork, showing in galleries and making art books. I'm contentedly doing abstract photographic artwork and writing.   Doug

ACKNOWLEDGEMENTS

I want to thank my wife, Marge, who listened patiently to every word of *Trial by Fire* and to Helane Freeman who designed and prepared this book for publication. I appreciate Carolyn Ryan for her meticulous editing and my original partner in this dramatic story, Gordon Ewert, without whom the pedestal house would never have been built. Thanks to Harry Heckendorf and John Diefenderfer the carpenter/contractors who skillfully made my pedestal house dream come true. I want to extend my gratitude toward my friend and general contractor, Roy Norvelle, whose former experience on thirteen Craig Ellwood houses made him perfect to build the second home. Thanks to Richard Gross who graciously donated his pedestal house negatives. *(See pictures 29, 30, 31, 32, and 33)*, and to Glen Allison whose photographs of my second house brought it so skillfully into the public eye. *(See pictures 101, 102, 103, 104, 106, 107, and 108)*. Thanks to Kenneth Nishimoto, my now diseased mentor, and to Bob Jackson the rendering expert who brought my *"creation"* into brilliant artistic existence. Also to artist, friend and neighbor, Dick Haines, for his musical history cartoon and painting, *Peasant Girl*, that brought a completion to our pedestal house. Thanks to my diseased wife Karon, and Lew Dominy, Steve Wooley, Craig Townsend, Toby Watson, Niel Dilworth, and Richard Sol, my draftsmen who worked to continue our practice. Appreciation goes to parents, Phil and Eva, my kids, Viveka, Lilianne, and Amanda and Marge's kids, Jenny, Katie, Christopher and Marggy. Oh yes, Daisy our beloved dog and, Ratface and Poo Bah, and all our cats.   Doug

OTHER BOOKS BY DOUG RUCKER

PERSONAL JOURNEY
How poetry forecast divorce

EARLY STORIES
Autobiography years 1927 thru 1950

GROUNDWORK
Autobiography years 1950 thru 1964

MOVING THROUGH
Poetry, 400 pages, years 1966 thru 1984

GROWING EDGE
Autobiography years 1964 thru 1970

BOOK OF WORDS
Sixty-seven homey essays

WHERE'S THE COOKIES AT?
Seventy-seven nonsensical essays

HAROLD AND THE ACID SEA OF REALITY
Sixty-eight essays on life

REFLECTIONS
Art - 25 color reflection photos with text

OFF THE WALL
Art - 25 digitally manipulated photos of graffiti

BRIEF BIOGRAPHY

After finishing the eighth grade in Chicago, Illinois, Doug was awarded a scholarship to the Chicago Art Institute. At Austin High School he played football and participated in sports on the track and swimming teams. He earned seven major letters while pursuing a three-year college preparatory course in architecture. At the University of Illinois in Champaign-Urbana he graduated with a Bachelor of Science degree in architecture and later worked as a draftsman in Denver, San Diego and Pasadena. In Altadena he married Karon Conan and received his California architectural license. In 1956, working for an excellent  architect with a smaller office in Brentwood Village, California, he created a partnership with two general contractors and built two houses for sale in Santa Monica Canyon. Selling the first and while finishing the second, the first came up for sale. He and Karon bought it and moved into their first home. Over four years Karon gave birth to three marvelous daughters. Meanwhile, Doug, with a partner was to build a *"dream house"* in Malibu for sale. Finished, the forty-two foot six inch square main floor floated on a pedestal thirty-five feet in the air with a wrap-around deck and views of the Malibu Creek estuary, Surfrider Beach, the Malibu movie colony and Serra Retreat. Halfway through the project his partner was forced to quit because of a sudden, severe illness that ultimately led to his early death. Because of the bad U. S. economy and having suddenly been struck with carrying three mortgages, the Ruckers were forced to sell their Santa Monica Canyon house, and finish and move into the Malibu house. He received much newspaper and magazine notoriety and lived in it four years before late in 1970 a brush fire burned it to the ground. By the end of 1972 Doug had built another more fire-resistant and equally dramatic house over the same foundations. It was similarly honored and published, but lost to a divorce in 1980. Doug is proud to say both houses were on the exclusive American Institute of Architect's Malibu Home Tours. In addition, the second house has been included since 1977 in Gebhard and Winter's, *An Architectural Guidebook to Los Angeles* including some of his peers, Frank Lloyd Wright, Richard Neutra, Frank Ghery, John Lautner, Quincy Jones, Thornton Abel, Craig Ellwood, Gordon Drake, etc. He is proud of his life work doing small homes and remodeling for fifty-four years in Malibu and up until retirement six years ago architecture has been the first and foremost focus of his life. Today he lives with his wife, Marjory Kron Lewi-Rucker, in the mountains above Malibu on an acre of land. He and his wife are enjoying a creative life of retirement both writing books and showing their artwork in local galleries.

www.ingramcontent.com/pod-product-compliance
Lightning Source LLC
Chambersburg PA
CBHW040801150426
42811CB00056B/1130